ENDORSEMENTS

My Dearest Brothers and Sisters, this book my dear friends, will give you insight to the power, purpose, and presence of the Holy Spirit. The incredible revelations of the workings of the Holy Spirit are invaluable to anyone who desires to be His vessel. My dear friend Dr. Michelle Corral has shared her personal experiences, demonstrating the move of the precious Holy Spirit upon the Body of Christ. I thoroughly recommend this book to all who wish to be used of God in these last days.

—PASTOR BENNY HINN

Secrets of the Anointing is God's solution to the agony of the human dilemma. May your heart be hungry to know that the Secret of the Anointing takes our inferior interior and makes it superior.

—BISHOP RON GIBSON

SECRETS *of the*
ANOINTING

SECRETS *of the* ANOINTING

— ◆ —

Walking in a Lifestyle of Holy Spirit Visitation

Dr. Michelle Corral

DESTINY IMAGE® PUBLISHERS, INC.
P.O. Box 310, Shippensburg, PA 17257-0310
"Promoting Inspired Lives."

This book and all other Destiny Image and Destiny Image Fiction books are available at Christian bookstores and distributors worldwide.

Cover design by Eileen Rockwell
Interior design by Terry Clifton

For more information on foreign distributors, call 717-532-3040.
Reach us on the Internet: www.destinyimage.com.

ISBN 13 TP: 978-0-7684-5070-5
ISBN 13 eBook: 978-0-7684-5071-2
ISBN 13 HC: 978-0-7684-5073-6
ISBN 13 LP: 978-0-7684-5072-9

For Worldwide Distribution, Printed in the U.S.A.
1 2 3 4 5 6 7 8 / 23 22 21 20 19

DEDICATION

Dedicated to my beloved husband, the Reverend Manuel Corral, my lifelong companion and best friend.

ACKNOWLEDGMENTS

I want to thank my beautiful granddaughters Gia and her sisters Sophia and Danielle for assisting me in this project. I also want to thank my dear assistant Icon Galang for her aid. I wish to acknowledge Vashia Rhone for assisting in the initial launch of the book and coordinating prayer. I also acknowledge the expertise and professionalism of my publishers and editor from Destiny Image Publishing.

CONTENTS

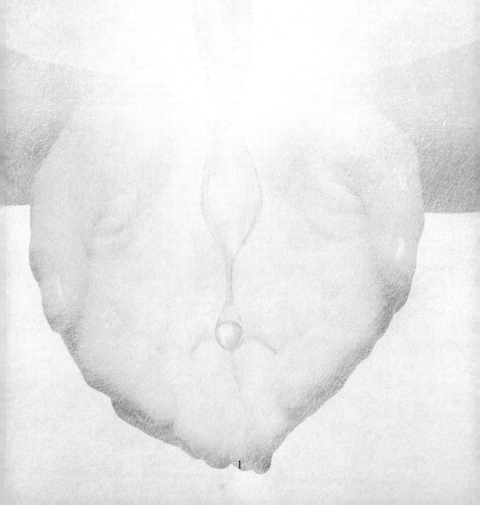

FOREWORD

If you look closely throughout the Bible, you can discern a divine pattern. It is always during some critical moment characterized by challenging circumstances that God executes His plan. He looks for a person willing to submit to Him, trust Him, and during the most adverse circumstances, He empowers that person with the divine enablement to overcome.

Ultimately, that individual embraces a particular burden as God's plan, purpose, and will for their life and through the leading and direction of the Spirit of God, feels morally compelled to act upon that revelation. This revelation becomes their vision, call, purpose, and mission. Such an individual is then in a position where they can be used to positively shape the course of humanity as change agents within their generation. Noah, Moses, Deborah, David, Esther, Mary, Paul the apostle, and many others were such individuals.

According to First Samuel 16:7, God does not look on the outward appearance. Instead, He looks at the heart of the individual. He looks for their willingness to yield their gifts, talents, and abilities to Him and consecrate them for His use.

The anointing ushers us into a realm of divine, supernatural power—the realm of *dunamis*. So many people, comparing themselves with others, have unfortunately disqualified themselves from being used by God because they feel they lack the right education, the right looks, the right connections, or any number of other false merits. But God does not select a person by such standards. First Corinthians 1:26-31 (KJV) states:

> *For ye see your calling, brethren, how that not many wise men after the flesh, not many mighty, not many noble, are called: but God hath chosen the foolish things of the world to confound the wise; and God hath chosen the weak things of the world to confound the things which are mighty; and base things of the world, and things which are despised, hath God chosen, yea, and things which are not, to bring to nought things that are: that no flesh should glory in his presence. But of him are ye in Christ Jesus, who of God is made unto us wisdom, and righteousness, and sanctification, and redemption: that, according as it is written, He that glorieth, let him glory in the Lord.*

These are challenging times. These are times of great controversy, uncertainty, complexity, and ambiguity. What the world needs is not people with more skill sets but people whose skill sets have been refined and consecrated to God by the anointing.

The anointing is a game-changer. David went from being a shepherd boy hidden in obscurity to one of Israel's greatest leaders because of the anointing. God is raising up individuals whom He is anointing to address the challenges of this world. God is raising up anointed individuals who: like the sons of Issachar are able to discern times and seasons; like Joseph are able to discern trends and engineer new economies while predicting future outcomes based on a particular course of action; like Esther are able to act decisively to save entire groups of people from impending ethnic cleansing; like Solomon are able to strategically mobilize fiscal and human resources and mastermind national policies that give rise to superpower nations; like Elijah are able to deliver countries from demonic oppression; and like Paul are able to preach the gospel on a global scale.

Throughout Scriptures we are given examples of many people who did incredible things because of the anointing. But the anointing is not just for biblical characters we admire; it is for contemporary believers. And it is not to be used to fulfill a personal agenda, but a divine agenda. The anointing connects the natural to the supernatural so that individuals do what they are neither capable of nor qualified to do without God. The anointing takes the struggle out of serving God and man.

The anointing ushers you into the flow of God's power so that you are able to do what your gifts are otherwise too crude to do; your education too insufficient to qualify you to do; and your network too feeble to support. Most people who are called struggle to truly maximize their potential because they lack the anointing. The anointing takes the struggle out of ministry, business, and day-to-day living. In this season, nothing will stop, stagnate, or limit you because of the anointing on your life.

Dr. Michelle Corral is one of these anointed persons. I have known her, admired her, and have been blessed by her anointed messages. But more than the messages, I have been inspired by her consecrated lifestyle and by the apostolic and prophetic grace upon her life. As I have watched, listened, pondered, and been blessed by Dr. Corral's teachings over the years, I have become increasingly intrigued by her insight and revelation. The anointing on her life is undeniably authentic, perceptibly pure, and beyond contamination. It is from this viewpoint that I am convinced she is the ideal person to reveal the secrets of the anointing. Her revelations are transformative, and she has paid a hefty price to impart a portion of her knowledge in her newest work, *The Secrets of the Anointing*.

This book is an invaluable investment of time and energy; it is an investment in the incalculable possibilities we may all secure when we choose to spend less time on the frivolous and more time mining the Word of God.

The anointing is still a mystery to many. Dr. Corral skillfully unpacks this vital and important message and shows us that the anointing is active and alive today within and through the believer. *The Secrets of the Anointing* is a practical guide to understanding the supernatural. It will help readers discover a path brimming with theological and prophetic significance. It is a literary GPS that guides the believer to a greater dimension of consecration and reliance upon the greatest empowerment specialist—the Holy Spirit Himself.

It's no coincidence that Dr. Corral has been charged with unveiling things that are hidden in plain view through this authoritative work. She is assigned to strategically open the mind and engage the spirit to a higher calling that has yet to be excavated—revealing a life of unlimited potential that awaits those who have the faith to sidestep the ordinary for God's extraordinary through the anointing of the Holy Spirit—God's instrument of empowerment.

The Holy Spirit has laid the groundwork for a new awakening in the Body of Christ and *The Secrets of the Anointing* is part of His strategy to equip the next generation of servant-leaders anointed by God to advance His Kingdom, to raise the standard of holiness, and to challenge their contemporaries not only to embrace Jesus as their Savior but also to become soulwinners in the process.

May *The Secrets of the* Anointing begin to quench your thirst for a greater relationship with the Holy Spirit as He anoints you to live a more victorious life. May His presence in your life open a door for you to be used to overcome the enemy and to influence personal and corporate revival within your spheres of influence. Indeed, it is *"Not by might, nor by power, but by my spirit, saith the Lord of hosts"* (Zechariah 4:6 KJV).

DR. CINDY TRIMM
Life-Strategist, Best-Selling Author, Humanitarian

Introduction

HOW GOD ANOINTED JESUS OF NAZARETH

How God anointed Jesus of Nazareth with the Holy Spirit and with power, who went about doing good and healing all who were oppressed of the devil, for God was with Him.

—Acts 10:38

SOME PEOPLE DESIRE THE ANOINTING, SOME LONG for it—but not enough to seek after it. Others know that they cannot live without it.

The anointing is one of the most sought-after, yet misunderstood subject matters in God's Word. Maybe you've heard of the anointing but don't know exactly what it is. The very explanation of Jesus' ministry is the anointing.

In every place the dust rose from His sandals there is demonstration of the anointing. As you will read in Chapter 1, Jesus' ministry is inaugurated by the sign of the Spirit—which is the anointing—and His mission is culminated in the anointing during His passion and resurrection.

The meaning of *Mashiach,* or Messiah, means "Anointed One" in Hebrew. In this book, I will uncover secrets throughout the Bible that will teach you about the anointing and how it operates. We will use the examples in the text of those whose lives were characterized by this incredible power.

You may ask the question, "Why do I need the anointing?" If you have ever pondered how to accomplish the dream you were put on this earth to do, you will realize it will happen through learning how to walk in the anointing.

I have written this book in a format beginning with the "Seven Avenues of Access." In Chapter 2, "The Protocols of Power," you will become proficient in the skills that are absolutely necessary in understanding the priorities of divine order. These are demonstrated scripturally through the position of the tribe of Levi in the camp of Israel and the place of the Ark of the Covenant. You will be able to inwardly perceive why Saul's kingdom failed and why David's prevailed.

In Chapters 3 and 4, I chose Joseph in his tribulations and Esther in her exaltation as model recipients of the anointing and how it works in our lives.

In Chapter 5, you will acquire the knowledge of how the anointing is transferable. I will teach you from the example of Jesus and His disciples before they received the baptism in the Spirit. Furthermore, I elaborate on the "contagious component" of the anointing. We will examine Moses and the seventy, and Joshua as the spiritual successor of Moses and why he was chosen for such an impartation.

In Chapter 6, I give you the tools to learn how to make the Holy Spirit your closest friend and companion. I teach you from the Word of God why this relationship is vital to the anointing.

In Chapter 7, I share with you one of the most essential purposes of the anointing and its power. We will discover the anointing and the power of His passion. I will reveal to you how the anointing consecrated and separated the work of the Cross above any of Jesus' other works in His three years of ministry. By this, you will understand how the anointing will empower you and separate you for your highest destiny.

At the end of every chapter, I include a prayer or prophetic word that God has given to me for you. I pray this book will enable you to ignite this generation and take you to the highest stratosphere of power possible.

Chapter 1

AVENUES OF ACCESS

I have found My servant David; with My holy oil I have anointed him.... The enemy shall not outwit him, nor the son of wickedness afflict him.

—Psalm 89:20,22

"The anointing of the Holy Spirit is given to illuminate His Word, to open the Scriptures, and to place the spiritual man in direct communication with the mind of God."

—Charles Fox Parham (1873–1929),
American Pentecostal Pioneer

It was a Sunday afternoon in 1972. After waiting in line with thousands of people, the time finally arrived. Throngs flooded through the door. Some were grasping their canes to stabilize their limps. Others were scurrying along swiftly with various types of breathing apparatus, yet a glimmer of hope beamed from their eyes. Even in this overwhelming anxiousness that almost became frantic, there was an unusual kindness and reverent courtesy shown toward one another.

What would it be like when someone who never walked could stand tall out of their wheelchair? I wondered how the mother of the little boy pushing the tiny walker would feel if her precious child could run and play like others.

As a bold, young adult and product of the greatest revival of the latter years of the 20th century, the "Jesus Movement," I had longed to experience again what I had recently felt the first time when I spoke in tongues. I came that day with the longing and expectation for the impossible to be a reality.

As the crowd was maneuvered through the doors, a kind usher filled with joy carefully directed me to the third balcony. I could hardly wait for the service to start. The gentle murmuring of 7,000 packed into the auditorium came to a halt. The moment the pianist struck the first note, it was as if time stopped. There was a sense of awe that swept across the multitude. Then suddenly, as if angels accompanied the choir, Miss Kuhlman appeared on the stage.

She seemed so tiny because I was so far away. As the stranger next to me offered his binoculars, Miss Kuhlman exclaimed, "Someone up in the third balcony is being healed of blindness." Suddenly for a flash of the moment, it seemed to turn darker than it was and instantly there appeared a slow-moving light that had the appearance of a lightning rod. It began to slowly make its way from one end of the row past my seat as it continued to travel. Then it paused. A boy who had been blind began exclaiming, "It's me! It's me!" As he was quickly rushed downstairs by a mother, many other miracles were happening throughout the upper level. When the service ended, I felt a strange sensation that lasted for hours. For the first time in my life, I experienced the anointing.

I went home that night thirsting and longing to relive the presence I had felt that Sunday afternoon in the Shrine auditorium. It was after that encounter with the anointing that I made up my mind that I would pay any price to experience it for the rest of my life.

Have you ever asked the question, "What is the anointing?" Perhaps you have experienced an overwhelming presence of God's power but were unclear how to identify it. It could have occurred in the most unlikely places or unusual circumstances. You may not have been in a church; it could have happened in a conversation discussing the things of God, like the two on the road to Emmaus:

They said to one another, "Did not our heart burn within us while He talked with us on the road, and while He opened the Scriptures to us? (Luke 24:32)

There may have been a miraculous moment when you sensed a gentle urge to do something for someone or be somewhere; and with it, there was an accompanied heavenly touch that undeniably witnessed to you *"This is the way, walk in it"* (Isaiah 30:21).

Maybe you wondered, *What was that feeling? Should I trust it?* My dear friend, if you belong to Jesus, and you are entirely His, you can be assured that the heavenly touch, or burning within your heart, is the anointing.

The most excellent example of what the anointing is and how it operates in someone's life is best demonstrated in the person of Jesus Christ who is God's anointed Messiah. Messiah *(Mashiach* in Hebrew) means "Anointed One."

Scripture identifies the Messiah with His unique identity and relationship with the Holy Spirit above all others:

Behold! My servant whom I uphold, My Elect One in whom My soul delights! I have put My Spirit upon Him; He will bring forth justice to the Gentiles (Isaiah 42:1).

The Scriptures foretold that the key identifying factor of the Messiah would be His unique relationship with the Holy Spirit. The Messiah would know the Holy Spirit as a Person, not just a power. Isaiah 61:1-3 foretells how the coming Messiah will be the first one to know Him as a person. It reads, *"The Spirit of the Lord God is upon Me because the Lord has anointed Me...He has sent Me to heal the brokenhearted..."* (Isaiah 61:1).

In a literal sense of Scripture, *"The Spirit of the Lord God"* is referred to as *"the Lord has anointed Me"* and *"He."* *"He has sent Me"* introduces the Spirit of God as a Person through the use of a personal pronoun.

The most significant human witness of who the Messiah is was John the Baptist (Matthew 11:11), yet Jesus said, *"I have a greater witness than John's"* (John 5:36). The greatest witness of who Jesus is and what His mission would be is the Holy Spirit. He proclaimed the identity of the Messiah as all of Israel waited for the unveiling of the One John had promised would be coming after him, yet at that time, John never saw Jesus or knew Him. It was only through the Spirit of God descending upon Jesus that John could know, "This is the One."

> *I did not know Him, but He who sent me to baptize with water said to me, "Upon whom you see the Spirit descending, and remaining on Him, this is He who baptizes with the Holy Spirit"* (John 1:33).

Think of it! John had proclaimed the coming of One he had never seen before. The mystery of it all was that John knew He was standing among them—but who was He?

John answered them saying, "I baptize with water, but there stands One among you whom you do not know" (John 1:26).

Which one among the multitudes was He? Who could He be among those who thronged daily to be baptized by John? John declared that he had no way of knowing Him, the One, in the natural. John 1:33 *"I did not know Him...."* John understood by the One who sent him to baptize, that he would know the One he had never seen before by *"the Spirit* [of God] *descending, and remaining on Him."*

Dear reader, the mission of the Holy Spirit is the same as it was thousands of years ago. He will reveal Jesus to you. He does this through the anointing. Before we journey into God's Word to see how He is going to release the anointing on your life, we will examine what I call the "anatomy of the anointing." This will help you understand what the anointing is and how it will affect your calling. The following are seven avenues of the anointing that will give you access to the Person and the power of the Holy Spirit in your life.

1. *The anointing is the bondage-breaking power of God.*

And it shall come to pass in that day, that his burden shall be taken away from off thy shoulder, and his yoke from off thy neck, and the yoke shall be destroyed because of the anointing (Isaiah 10:27 KJV).

Throughout Scripture, the text teaches that the yoke is a symbol of servitude and bondage. In biblical times when an ox was subservient to the plowman by not resisting his lead, the neck of the ox would become enlarged due to the thick fat around the tissues. The fat in the neck was because the ox did not resist the pull of the plow. On the other hand, a lean-necked beast under the yoke meant it used muscle to turn in the opposite direction of its master's lead. As a result, an ox that was lean or stiff-necked had no fat.

The fat is a type of anointing with a substance like oil. When the animal would comply, its neck became so large from the fat that the yoke would burst, likening the anointing. The prophet Isaiah likens our yielding to the Holy Spirit to an oxen's neck that has become so fat with the oil that the bonds burst.

2. *The anointing will make you the personal possession of the Holy Spirit.*

> *I have found My servant David; with My holy oil have I anointed him* (Psalm 89:20).

When we become anointed, there is a profoundly intimate relationship with the Holy Spirit that causes us to become His personal possession. We know that everyone who has received Christ as their personal Lord and Savior belongs to Him. However, the anointing is designated for every part of our entire being to be wholly surrendered and submitted to whatever the Holy Spirit prompts or requests of us.

You become His treasured possession because now His power has set you aside for a purpose, not of this world. You are *in* the world, but not *of* this world. In the book of Psalms, the concept of possession is expressed, which uses personal pronouns referring to God when referring to His anointed children:

- God shows..."*mercy to His anointed*" (Psalm 18:50).

- The Lord..."*saves His anointed*" (Psalm 20:6).

- *The Almighty declares...*"*I have ordained a lamp for mine anointed*" (Psalm 132:17 KJV).

In each of these verses, God is assuring us that when we receive His anointing we are His personal possession and treasure. This is why the Word says, *"Do not touch My anointed ones, and do My prophets no harm"* (Psalm 105:15).

The anointing oil of Exodus 30:23-33 was used to separate and consecrate whatever it touches unto God.

...This shall be an holy anointing oil **unto me** *throughout your generations* (Exodus 30:31 KJV).

"Unto me" means exclusively belonging to God, and is set apart for no other purpose but His purpose.

3. *The anointing will turn your darkest day into destiny.*

> *Thus says the Lord to His anointed, to Cyrus...I will give you the treasures of darkness and hidden riches of secret places...* (Isaiah 45:1,3).

The *"treasures of darkness"* are the very things the enemy thought to use to destroy you, yet God uses to deploy you into purpose. Like the day Joseph was sold into slavery by his brothers became God's plan of purpose in his life. For Joseph, the day of darkness, tears, shock, and trauma became a design of destiny. At the time, Joseph had no idea he was sent to Egypt to become second to Pharaoh.

The sign of the Holy Spirit in Joseph's life as the interpreter of dreams caused Pharaoh to say, *"Can we find such a one as this, a man in whom is the Spirit of God? ...there is no one as discerning and wise as you"* (Genesis 41:38-39).

4. *The anointing will bring divine liberation and exultation over the enemy.*

> *You prepare a table before me in the presence of my enemies; You anoint my head with oil; my cup runs over* (Psalm 23:5).

Did you know the anointing prepares a platform in the presence of your enemies? When the oil is placed with another liquid substance, it always rises; this reveals by nature the work of the anointing in our lives. Do you know the anointing will lift you in the presence of your enemies? This means the enemy can never exact harm upon you. Let me give you an example. In biblical times, kings were anointed. The anointing was a symbol of power exclusively on the king to triumph over the enemies of Israel: *"Then Samuel took a vial of oil, and poured it upon his head, and kissed him, and said, Is it not because the Lord hath anointed thee to be captain over his inheritance?"* (1 Samuel 10:1 KJV).

Our enemies may not be physical, but demonic in nature. As children of God, we should never resort to revenge, or repay evil with evil. We are called to love our enemies and overcome evil with good (Romans 12:17-21). When we follow this path of power, we can be assured that *"No weapon formed against you shall prosper"* (Isaiah 54:17).

5. *The anointing will bring you restoration after devastation.*

I want to take you to one of the most exceptional exemplifications of how the anointing can transform a life. It is the biblical account of King David and Mephibosheth. Let's go to Second Samuel 4:4:

> *Jonathan, Saul's son, had a son who was lame in his feet. He was five years old when the news about Saul and Jonathan came from Jezreel; and his nurse took him up and fled. And it happened, as she made haste to flee, that he fell and became lame. His name was Mephibosheth.*

Frantically, they hurried and fled for their lives. The nurse gathered up the little prince into her arms. His legs dangled to her knees as she managed to wrap his royal shawl around his shoulders. Then, as her rapid steps gained momentum, the cape she so tightly bundled around him unraveled and fell to the ground. Together, they fell. Injuries to him were insurmountable. That very hour, Mephibosheth lost his land, his legacy, and the use of his legs.

Scripture begins the introduction to Jonathan's son with the record of the traumatic losses that took place in one day. The text is not designed just to give us a historical account of the events that took place. Scripture reveals these events so anyone who has suffered traumatic loses like Mephibosheth will know there is hope, healing, and deliverance available.

If we follow the chronicles of time recorded in this account, Mephibosheth's is a story of tragedy to triumph. In Second Samuel chapter 9, God's Word records a transformation and miraculous restoration through his encounter with the anointing.

To illustrate this to you, if we follow what is written in order of occurrence, the next time we read about Mephibosheth in Scripture, he is an adult. We don't know exactly what happened after that woeful day when his nurse fled with him, but we are told that he is living in a secluded place of isolation called Lo Debar. The following passage is found in Second Samuel 9:1-4:

> *Now David said, "Is there still anyone who is left of the house of Saul, that I may show him kindness for Jonathan's sake?"*

And there was a servant of the house of Saul whose name was Ziba. So when they had called him to David, the king said to him, "Are you Ziba?"

He said, "At your service!"

Then the king said, "Is there not still someone of the house of Saul, to whom I may show the kindness of God?"

And Ziba said to the king, "There is still a son of Jonathan who is lame in his feet."

So the king said to him, "Where is he?"

And Ziba said to the king, "Indeed he is in the house of Machir the son of Ammiel, in Lo Debar."

There are two spiritually significant meanings to this place: Lo Debar translated from Hebrew to English means "without word," this can also mean "not having." The meaning of this place helps us to understand that Mephibosheth was not just in a physical location but in *emotional isolation* as well.

It was not until King David inquired, *"Is there anyone who is left of the house of Saul, that I may show him kindness for Jonathan's sake,"* that Mephibosheth was discovered.

King David is God's anointed. There is no other in the Hebrew Scriptures who is associated with the word "anointed" as many times as the son of Jesse. First, David is anointed by the prophet Samuel in First Samuel 16:13. Second, David experiences another anointing publicly in Second Samuel 2:4. Third, David is anointed as king of Israel in Second Samuel 5:3. Scripture gives him a title greater than king; it acclaims him as the anointed of God.

Mephibosheth has to muster all his strength to respond to the call of the king. Though he was lame, he still said, "Yes, I will go." Some of us have *disabilities* that God sees as *abilities* to make us more dependent on the Holy Spirit for everything. Nothing held Mephibosheth back from responding to the king's call. This illustrates that when he came near David, he came near the anointing.

The miracle of restoration after years of devastation are a parallel of what the anointing will do in your life. David said to Mephibosheth:

> *Do not fear, for I will surely show you kindness*
> *for Jonathan your father's sake, and will restore*
> *to you all the land of Saul your grandfather;*
> *and you shall eat bread at my table continually*
> (2 Samuel 9:7).

If we closely examine this verse, we will see the effects of the anointing. First, there will be restoration of the land. David said he would restore to him all the land of Saul his grandfather. In a literal sense, this meant Mephibosheth, who was living in abject poverty in Lo Debar, would experience a complete restoration of all properties owned by King Saul. These were parcels of land and houses owned by Saul,

Jonathan, and the royal family. In one day, God restored Mephibosheth's land.

Second, this also meant the return would not just be land, it would also be legacy: *"and you shall eat bread at my table continually."* To eat bread at the king's table was a privilege enjoyed only by his sons and daughters. This meant the restoration process would include being someone of special status. Through the anointing, God brought a restoration of ruins.

If you say yes, the anointing will fall on you as it did on Mephibosheth. As you serve, the anointing increases because it is given for service. Restoration after tribulation is an effect of the bondage-breaking power in the anointing.

6. *The anointing will stir the power of what is prophetic in you.*

> *But this is what was spoken by the prophet Joel: "And it shall come to pass in the last days, says God, That I will pour out of My Spirit on all flesh; your sons and your daughters shall prophesy, your young men shall see visions, your old men shall dream dreams"* (Acts 2:16-17).

On the day of Pentecost, the sign of the Spirit upon all flesh is that the Holy Spirit would be poured out on sons and daughters who would prophesy. In a Hebrew sense of Scripture, this means that a particular form of prophecy given would be in dreams. Numbers 12:6 says, *"...If there is a prophet among you, I, the Lord, make Myself known to him in a vision; I will speak to him in a dream."*

One of the promises of Pentecost is that there would be an outpouring of God's personal messages to His people by visions of the night or dreams:

> But **the anointing** which you have received from Him **abides in you**, and you do not need that anyone teach you; but as **the same anointing teaches you** concerning all things, and is true, and is not a lie, and just as it has taught you, you will abide in Him (1 John 2:27).

The abiding anointing is resident in every believer; it works within you to teach you how to receive the personal message God has for you at any time, whenever He chooses. Sometimes His word comes in the night to give direction or divine protection through warnings.

You are so precious to your heavenly Father that He knows your sorrows, troubles, and anxieties. He lets you know how personal He is with every detail of your life by giving dreams. He gave Jacob a dream when he was filled with fear and running from the face of Esau, his brother. The tender compassion of His heavenly Father comforted Jacob in his exile out of the land by giving him a dream of a ladder coming down from Heaven with the angels of God ascending and descending upon it (Genesis 28:10-12).

In Genesis 28:18, Jacob woke up out of his dream and poured oil on the rock he used for a pillow. The oil was the symbol of the anointing that brings God's personal prophetic message to you.

Then Jacob rose early in the morning, and took the stone that he had put at his head, set it up as a pillar, and poured oil on top of it (Genesis 28:18).

You are so precious to your heavenly Father that He knows your sorrows, troubles, and anxieties.

7. *The least expected is the one elected for the anointing.*

Then Samuel took the horn of oil, and anointed him [David] *in the midst of his brothers...* (1 Samuel 16:13).

Have you ever been through an excruciating experience that devastated your life? You may wonder, *Why did I have to go through this?* Trials on a continuous basis can make us feel empty and without hope. Some of us may feel as if we are the last in line to receive our breakthrough.

You must not realize you are the candidate the Holy Spirit is looking for to use for the glory of God. Let me explain. In First Samuel 16, the text teaches that God had chosen someone never expected to be Israel's next king. As the prophet filled his horn with oil, he was sent to confirm God's election in the midst of rejection. The text documents the details as Samuel bids Jesse to call all of his sons.

As the sacrifice was offered, and the banquet prepared, all seven of Jesse's sons were called to this most honorable event, but one. As Samuel scrutinized and passed before each of the young men, he said to Jesse, *"The Lord has not chosen these"* (1 Samuel 16:10). Bewildered, Samuel said to Jesse, *"Are all the young men here?"* And Jesse said, *"There remains yet the youngest, and there he is, keeping the sheep."* And Samuel said to Jesse, *"Send and bring him. For we will not sit down till he comes here"* (1 Samuel 16:11).

You are the candidate the Holy Spirit is looking for to use for the glory of God.

In a Hebrew sense of Scripture, the word "youngest" used in this passage is the word *qatan*. The word *qatan* can mean younger, but it also can mean "least." We know it did not mean "youngest" of all because in First Samuel 17:12, the reference refers to Jesse as the father of eight sons. However, First Chronicles 2:15 teaches us that in birth order, David was the seventh son of Jesse, not the eighth, which would have made him the youngest.

The question arises, for such an awesome, once-in-a-life-time experience of having the prophet come to their house and prepare a banquet, why wasn't David at the table with the rest of the family?

It appears the context conveys to us that David was the *qatan* of the family—the one least expected was God's elected to be the king.

Beloved, these things were written not so we would be experts in Hebrew history, but to demonstrate God's validation and affirmation for every person who feels like the *qatan,* the least or the one you have forgotten. I believe it was from this experience that David wrote Psalm 23.

How unjust for David not to be called to the table. He was the only one of Jesse's sons not invited to participate in the most memorable event of their family's history. What reasons could even slightly justify such a great honor as having Samuel the prophet call your family to the sacrifice and the meal and not be invited?

The following verses from First Samuel 17 give us insight into the level of apparent animosity David's brothers had toward him:

- *"Now David was the son of that Ephrathite of Bethlehem Judah, whose name was Jesse; and who had eight sons"*... (1 Samuel 17:12).

- *"David was the* [qatan]. *And the three oldest followed Saul"* (1 Samuel 17:14).

- *"Now Eliab his oldest brother heard when he spoke to the men; and Eliab's anger was aroused against David, and he said, 'Why did you come down here? And with whom have you left those few sheep in the wilderness? I know your pride and the insolence of your heart, for you have come down to see the battle'"* (1 Samuel 17:28).

- *"And David said, 'What have I now done? Is there not a cause?'"* (1 Samuel 17:29).

Beloved, please remember that everything recorded in Scripture is the living prophetic word for every generation. What appears to be a historical narrative is meant to confront every person who has been thorough isolation and the feeling of desperation in the moments when the excruciating experience of rejection is targeted at us.

The coronation of David as king shows us how the least expected is the one God elected for purpose and promise. The coronation of David shows us the least expected is the one selected for the anointing. Throughout Scriptures, the text teaches that it was the one that man rejected whom God elected for His glory.

Beloved, do not let the pain of your past hold you hostage to what people think of you. God has promised that He will give you beauty for brokenness.

The day of his anointing was the time God prepared a table before him in the presence of his enemies.

You prepare a table before me in the presence of my enemies; You anoint my head with oil; my cup runs over (Psalm 23:5).

Just as the Lord prepared a banquet on that day that began in grief but shifted into greatness for David, so shall the anointing break the bondage of rejection and personal pain that will launch you into your highest dimension of destiny.

> ## God has promised that He will give you beauty for brokenness.

Prayer for Avenues of Access to the Anointing

Dear Holy Spirit,

I ask that You would activate all seven areas of access to the anointing in my life. I believe that the same power You poured upon every generation of the past You will pour upon me. Use me beyond my comprehension and teach me how to always surrender to You. Amen.

Chapter 2

THE PROTOCOLS
OF POWER

*Again, the kingdom of heaven is like treasure
hidden in a field, which a man found and
hid; and for joy over it he goes and sells all
that he has and buys that field.*

—Matthew 13:44

I T COSTS MUCH, BUT IT IS WORTH THE COST...IT COSTS everything," Kathryn Kuhlman said, "It's what you want most that you are willing to pay the price for." I can still hear her voice like echoes in the wind. These were the words that carried me through some of the toughest times and distressing days of ministry.

Many of us, when desiring to buy something, will try to find it at a lower price. However, when it is something we found that we long for more than anything else, we are willing to pay any price for it.

You may have made the decision, and said, "I want to be used of God; I am willing to do whatever it takes." Let me tell you about the price behind the power that God desires to lavish upon you. I can assure you, whatever we give Him is not worthy to be compared to the glory that will be revealed in us.

> *For I consider that the sufferings of this present time are not worthy to be compared with the glory which shall be revealed in us* (Romans 8:18).

Now I want to share with you a personal experience revealing how the anointing is worth anything the Lord asks of you.

Many years ago when I first began in ministry, I had a burning desire to evangelize in the People's Republic of China. Missionary stories of the brave and fearless who had been imprisoned and sentenced to hard labor, inspired me to dare to tread in that forbidden frontier. In 1980 the Chinese government proposed a plan to begin to develop a friendship with the West.

After years of silence and no official communication from China with the West, I seized the opportunity to plan a Bible-smuggling mission to assist the underground believers. Divine providence arranged that in the summer I would preach in a series of healing crusades in the Philippines, so I decided then to prepare our move into the dangerous and uncharted waters of the People's Republic of China.

Thirty volunteers joined me on this mission tour. Each one bravely desired to also smuggle Bibles for the suffering believers in the underground Christian church. To execute the task efficiently in a most excellent way for God, we submitted ourselves to training with an international missionary organization closely connected to the underground church. They advised us not to let everyone be carriers of the Bibles in the group. For a mission this dangerous, they suggested we select keen, brave, calm individuals who would not fret under the threat of interrogation and search by the communist customs agents.

After a season of training in how to conduct ourselves should the inevitable searching of our bags happen, we set out on the mission to Manila, Hong Kong, and the People's Republic of China.

The anointing was heavy while we were in Manila. During the healing crusades, a young boy who was stricken with polio—one leg like a stick—walked and ran in the service. Hundreds gave their lives to Christ as a result of witnessing His healing power.

As I packed my suitcase before leaving Manila for Hong Kong, I felt the Holy Spirit prompt me to look very secular, unlike a missionary, when I arrived in Hong Kong. I felt His nudging to put cosmetics, false eyelashes, and other similar items on top of my clothing as I packed—underneath were the hidden treasures and gems of God's Word, concealed before arriving on the mainland.

EQUIPPED BY THE HOLY SPIRIT

Though I experienced the anointing so powerfully in Manila, I sensed the closeness of the Holy Spirit equipping me for China in a way I never felt before. There was a boldness and bravery given for this occasion. He made us willing to lay down our lives no matter the cost. With that "price" however, I had no idea what miracles I was about to witness.

Beloved, when you are willing to do whatever it takes, there is no limit nor can it equal the power and demonstration He will lavish upon you in return. It cannot be compared to the glory within us (Romans 8:18).

As we boarded the hydroplane from Kowloon to Canton, and although the cities are so close together, it felt so far away because of our mission. I'm not sure if the nausea I felt was from the rocky ride across the sea or my heart pounding in my ribcage in regard to what may await us. When my feet touched the land, I quickly searched for my bags. I rushed to identify my suitcase so I could safeguard my bundled treasures hidden under the garments.

At first glance at the surroundings, it all seemed like a dream out of the past. The dilapidated buildings in front of us and the chiming of bicycle bells off in the distance made it feel like I was taken back in time.

Before I knew it, I was inside the customs area. A tall, thin man dressed in olive green military garb approached me. The red star on his cap emphasized he was in Mao Zedong's regime. The soldier's face was trained to show no emotion. He glared at me without expression and pointed to the long, lowered counter where I was to lift my luggage. I comforted myself with the thought, *Some people appear to be going through without difficulty, maybe I can escape without opening my suitcase.* Suddenly, I was told to open it.

As the guard began to scrutinize my belongings, my heart sunk and my knees actually began to knock. I could feel the adrenaline rush through my body. He called another guard over and they started to whisper in Mandarin to each other, staring at me. They were mesmerized by the false eyelashes and were in awe at the nail polish and cosmetics. This is because I entered into the country in the early stages of negotiating with the Western world after years of silence. These men had never seen these types of items before.

I came prepared for the worst, thinking they were studying me because they were going to take me in. Much to my surprise, they shut the suitcase and with smiles on their faces directed me to the exit. Miraculously, our Bibles were not discovered and were safely retrieved by brethren in the underground. The wisdom God gave me through the anointing to arrange my suitcase according to the leading of the Spirit the way I did threw them off guard. This was just the beginning of the miracles that were to follow.

FRIENDSHIP EXCHANGE

On Sunday, a prior arrangement had been made for a "friendship exchange" at the 3 Self Patriotic Church. I was warned to present my message within the bounds of the Chinese government's nonnegotiable regulations. I had to stay within the boundaries because the interpreter, a communist, would never allow the news of the gospel to be freely preached.

I felt so grieved in my heart knowing that there would be hundreds of precious Chinese souls who never heard the gospel—yet now was the moment of opportunity, but how? Even if I boldly proclaimed it, the government interpreter would never translate what I was saying.

In the friendship exchange, some of the volunteers with me got up to speak to the large, awaiting crowd. All that prevented us from being able to reach them was the language and, of course, the strict rules that were enforced by the 3 Self Patriotic Church.

After the service, the congregation began to gather in the courtyard to greet us with gestures of kindness and courtesy, but not with speech, because we could not speak nor understand each other's languages.

Dear Jesus, if I could speak Mandarin, I could preach to them and tell them about You, I thought to myself. The brave missionaries who had been chosen in the group to participate in smuggling Bibles also felt the longing to speak to these people. I remembered how on the day of Pentecost the 120 left the upper room after being baptized in the Spirit and spoke in tongues and dialects to the people in Jerusalem in languages they never studied.

Suddenly, one small woman approached me; I felt such compassion for her yet felt so helpless. I had no way to tell her that Jesus loved her. We had traveled thousands of miles and risked our lives for this opportunity. *"Jesus,"* I prayed, *"Let me tell this precious lady about Your love for her."* As I opened my mouth to speak, it was not English that came out. It sounded like a Chinese dialect I never heard before. The others who bravely brought in the Bibles also begin to speak in a Chinese dialect. This lasted for about six or seven minutes. Lines began to quickly form as the Chinese started to converse with us and touching themselves, outwardly demonstrating that they were requesting prayer for hurting parts of their bodies.

Then the government official who spoke English rushed over and agitatedly broke up what began to be a healing service. He motioned to us to go into a private room and said, "No one is allowed to be baptized." He proceeded to make us write our names on a tablet and hurried us to our bus. I can only vaguely remember what he said because the anointing was so present that it did not lift for days. Miraculously, no harm came upon us.

You have been destined for the anointing.

DESTINED FOR THE ANOINTING

Beloved, the same Holy Spirit who empowered us for the impossible during those few moments to speak the gospel to the precious people living in China is the same Holy Spirit who will fill you with His anointing. I know what God did for me, God will do for you. You have been destined for the anointing.

Dear friend, in the final portion of this chapter, I want to teach you one of the most important primary principles about the anointing. It is an essential precept in learning how to surrender self to the Holy Spirit. I call this precept the "Protocols of Power."

A protocol is a formal procedure that requires adherence to a superior. The anointing should be placed in a position of height and priority in our lives. This means, in the language of protocol, we esteem it as a treasure—a pearl of great price.

The way this protocol operates is by understanding it must be first above all other things in life.

> *Again, the kingdom of heaven is like a merchant seeking beautiful pearls, who, when he had found one pearl of great price, went and sold all that he had and bought it* (Matthew 13:45-46).

First, the anointing can be likened to the Ark of the Covenant in ancient Israel. The Ark was perceived as the Holy of Holies. When the children of Israel were wandering in the wilderness for forty years, the Ark was in the center of the tribes positioned in the tabernacle.

However, when the children of Israel moved out of the desert into their destined Promised Land, God commanded that the Ark be moved out of the center into the forefront. This is a prophetic parallel to understanding the priority that the anointing must have in our lives as we enter into our Promised Land.

> *Then Joshua spoke to the priests, saying, "Take up the ark of the covenant and cross over before the people." So they took up the ark of the covenant and went before the people* (Joshua 3:6).

David's life is a perfect example of the protocols of power. The first national gathering of his reign as a monarch over all of Israel was to establish God as King—not himself. To David, placing the Ark in the position of highest priority was his greatest achievement as king. This was something

Saul never considered or sought after. The Ark, representing God's throne, power, and anointing, was not on the agenda of Saul's achievements as king. Sadly, it was just the opposite. God's anointing, presence, power, and throne were not priorities for Saul.

> *And let us bring the ark of our God back to us,*
> *for we have not inquired at it since the days of*
> *Saul* (1 Chronicles 13:3).

First Chronicles 13:3 is comparing and contrasting the difference between Saul's kingdom and David's, consequently telling us why David's dynasty is the one with the anointing. David's holy bloodline will last forever as the Messiah sits on His throne. On the contrary, Saul's rulership lasted only twenty years. First Samuel 13:1 illustrates that in those twenty years, only two were blessed with the anointing.

Contrary to David's quest to set up the Ark as the most important priority of His kingdom, Saul left the Ark at a secluded distance, hidden away in a place called Kirjath Jearim:

> *So it was that the ark remained in Kirjath*
> *Jearim a long time; it was there twenty years.*
> *And all the house of Israel lamented after the*
> *Lord* (1 Samuel 7:2).

Let's glimpse the true heart of David who was established as God's anointed.

Immediately after becoming king, David conquers Jebusite territory and becomes the founder of Jerusalem. The establishment of Jerusalem was to turn the former strongholds into a sanctuary by placing the Ark in a position of priority. Scripture elaborates on the details of this event because it is the secret behind David's success. David's concern was to *"bring up"* the Ark. To bring it up refers to elevating it to a position of precedence and priority.

> *And David gathered all Israel together to Jerusalem, to **bring up the ark of the Lord** to its place, which he had prepared for it* (1 Chronicles 15:3).

Let me give you one more example of the protocols of power, and how the anointing must be placed in a position of priority.

In ancient Israel, during the blistering days and freezing cold nights in the wilderness, the Almighty covered Israel with His cloud of glory. The glory of the Lord protected and directed them in the form of a cloud as they wandered through the wilderness.

> *Now on the day that the tabernacle was raised up, the cloud covered the tabernacle, the tent of the Testimony; from evening until morning it was above the tabernacle like the appearance of fire. So it was always: the cloud covered it by day, and the appearance of fire by night. Whenever the cloud was taken up from above the tabernacle, after that the children of Israel*

*would journey; and in the place where the
cloud settled, there the children of Israel would
pitch their tents. At the command of the Lord
the children of Israel would journey, and at
the command of the Lord they would camp; as
long as the cloud stayed above the tabernacle
they remained encamped. Even when the cloud
continued long, many days above the tabernacle,
the children of Israel kept the charge of the
Lord and did not journey.*

*So it was, when the cloud was above the tabernacle a few days: according to the command of the
Lord they would remain encamped, and according to the command of the Lord they would
journey. So it was, when the cloud remained
only from evening until morning: when the
cloud was taken up in the morning, then they
would journey; whether by day or by night,
whenever the cloud was taken up, they would
journey. Whether it was two days, a month,
or a year that the cloud remained above the
tabernacle, the children of Israel would remain
encamped and not journey; but when it was
taken up, they would journey. At the command
of the Lord they remained encamped, and at the
command of the Lord they journeyed; they kept
the charge of the Lord, at the command of the
Lord by the hand of Moses* (Numbers 9:15-23).

In conclusion, I want to emphasize two valuable ways we can incorporate the protocols of power by understanding the ministry of the Levites.

One of the ways the glory remained among the Israelites was through the sacrificial service of the Levites. Levi, the father of this tribe, was the third born son of Jacob and Leah. His mother named him by prophetic inspiration of the Holy Spirit. Leah was given the insight to see his destiny. Levi means "attached" or "to be joined."

> *She conceived again and bore a son, and said, "Now this time my husband will become attached to me, because I have borne him three sons." Therefore his name was called Levi* (Genesis 29:34).

By the Spirit of God, Leah was able to foresee the future of Levi's descendants. The name she gave him defines the destiny of "attaching" Heaven and earth.

This would be done by the Levites' unique calling among the tribes of Israel. Their lives of consecration and separation would be the means by which the glory cloud would descend and remain upon the children of Israel during their days in the desert.

The First Protocol of Power: Separation

Separation means not all things are the same. To make holy also means to "separate." In the book of Acts, after much fasting and prayer, the Holy Spirit "separated" Saul and Barnabas for their designated destinies.

> As they ministered to the Lord, and fasted, the Holy Spirit said, "Now separate to Me Barnabas and Saul for the work to which I have called them" (Acts 13:2).

> But when it pleased God, who separated me from my mother's womb, and called me through His grace (Galatians 1:15).

Likewise, we see the illustration of this separation in the Levites.

In Numbers chapter 1, the Levites were excluded from the national census, which meant their census, though part of the same nation, had to be taken separately. This was because the Levites were appointed for what only was anointed. They were given a mission of ministry over the tabernacle.

> But the Levites were not numbered among them by their fathers' tribe.... Only the tribe of Levi you shall not number, nor take a census of them among the children of Israel (Numbers 1:47,49).

Next, the Levites could not pitch their tents in the same area within the camp as the other tribes. The protocols of power required that this separation be a public illustration through the positioning of their tents around the tabernacle.

This concept prophetically prefigures how we can abide in God's presence 24/7 at the asking.

Their tents had to be located directly under the cloud of glory *"round about the tabernacle"* (Numbers 1:50 KJV).

> *But the Levites shall camp around the tabernacle of the Testimony, that there may be no wrath on the congregation of the children of Israel; and the Levites shall keep charge of the tabernacle of the Testimony* (Numbers 1:53).

The Levites' separation involved a consecration that brought Heaven down to earth. It was because of their sacrificial service that the cloud maintained and remained among the children of Israel.

We must handle our ministries with care and personal prayer.

The Second Protocol of Power: Designation

The Levites express precedence in separation and *designation*. Not all of the Levitical responsibilities were the same. One of the most important assignments was in carrying the tabernacle in the wilderness.

How the tabernacle was carried prophetically prefigures how the anointing must be handled in the protocols of power.

To illustrate this, Numbers chapter 4 is dedicated to the designation of the Levites' service according to protocol. For example, the Kohathites were charged with carrying the sanctuary: *"This is the service of the sons of Kohath in the tabernacle of meeting, relating to the most holy things"* (Numbers 4:4). They were given specific instructions about how to carry *"the most holy things."* The sanctuary items they would carry could not be put on a cart. They had to be *personally* carried on a bar like the Ark. This prophetically prefigures how we must handle our ministries with care and personal prayer.

All of the furnishings and items of the sanctuary to be carried on the shoulders of the sons of Kohath were anointed with holy anointing oil as described in Exodus 40. When Moses set up the tabernacle, the text teaches even the setup of these items had to be positioned in protocol and divine order. In Exodus 40:3, the first item to be placed in the tabernacle was the Ark. This is because it had the highest priority.

And you shall take the anointing oil, and anoint the tabernacle and all that is in it; and you shall hallow it and all its utensils, and it shall be holy. You shall anoint the altar of the burnt offering and all its utensils, and consecrate the altar. The altar shall be most holy (Exodus 40:9-10).

If we examine the setup of the tabernacle, nothing could be anointed in it until it was set in its proper place according to the divine order and protocol. There is a repetitive pattern in the text:

*You shall bring in the table and arrange the things that are to be **set in order** on it; and you shall bring in the lampstand and light its lamps. You shall also **set** the altar of gold for the incense before the ark of the Testimony, and put up the screen for the door of the tabernacle* (Exodus 40:4-5).

All of these specific instructions teach us there is a protocol. When the protocol is in place, then the power is released. It was not until everything was set exactly as God ordered it, *then* Moses took the anointing oil and anointed all that was in it (Exodus 40:9).

This demonstrates in our personal lives how positioning everything in proper order brings the anointing to its highest immensity and greatest intensity.

In summary, when we understand these prophetic precepts, we can clearly understand designation. The Kohathites could not put these items in or move them the same way the curtains or the boards were transported. In contrast, the sons of Gershon had the charge over the curtains, and the sons of Merari were appointed to the boards and pillows that were in transference by cart (Numbers 4:24-26,29-33). We must learn to separate and designate.

Beloved, let us put the protocols of power into practice in our lives and ministries.

Prayer for the Protocols of Power

Dear Holy Spirit,

Teach me how to place the anointing as a priority in my life. I will never consider it second place. I treasure this gift as the pearl of great price in my life. Teach me, like David, the secrets of success that come from honoring You, Your leading, and Your guidance as the most important treasures on earth. Amen.

Chapter 3

THE CONFERRING
OF THE COAT

Now Israel loved Joseph more than all his children, because he was the son of his old age: and he made him a coat of many colours.
—Genesis 37:3 (KJV)

"The power of the Holy Ghost came down like a cloud. It was brighter than the sun. I was covered and wrapped in it. I was baptized with the Holy Ghost and fire and power, which has never left me."
—MARIA WOODWORTH ETTER
(1844-1924), American Healing Evangelist

HAVE YOU EVER QUESTIONED WHAT GAVE JOSEPH the strength to survive such perilous ordeals in his life? At age seventeen, he was trafficked into slavery. By the time he was thirty, his word had ruled over the most extensive empire on earth.

Think of it! How could Joseph possibly arise so resilient after a brutal betrayal that orchestrated his kidnapping? Was there a secret to the success in his life that becomes apparent even before he is appointed viceroy over the land of Egypt?

One of the most intriguing passages in the Joseph narrative has raised a question in my mind for years. How can he be "prosperous" when he was a slave and lost everything? The indication conveyed in the context of the previous verses in Genesis 37 is that the sale masterminded by his brothers brought him to the lowest place of his life—and is why the word "pit" is used seven times.

Moses, the author of Genesis, uses this word with superfluity deliberately. It is used as an introduction to Genesis 39. Moses wanted us to understand that in the natural it was impossible in Joseph's circumstances to experience continual triumph after so many tragedies.

Now Joseph had been taken down to Egypt. And Potiphar, an officer of Pharaoh, captain of the guard, an Egyptian, bought him from the

Ishmaelites who had taken him down there.
The Lord was with Joseph, *and he was a successful man; and he was in the house of his master the Egyptian* (Genesis 39:1-2).

The text is designed for us to see that there is an unstoppable surge of success that continuously emerges out of the most grievous circumstances in Joseph's life. Scripture presents a pattern that indicates the comeback after an unseen power is aiding Joseph through every crisis. That power is the anointing.

First, the anointing is the primary principle behind Joseph's ability to keep rising. He literally is taken out of the prison, which in biblical times was referred to as a pit, to the palace in one day.

The Anointing and the Conferring of the Coat

The conferring of the coat is placed center stage as the dramatic events unfold before the sale of Joseph to the Ishmaelites. There is a streamlined similitude that foreshadows the anointing and through "the coat" throughout the Word of God. Let's look at the evidence prefigured in Exodus.

For Aaron's sons thou shalt make coats, and thou shalt make for them girdles, and bonnets shalt thou make for them, for glory and for beauty. And thou shalt put them upon Aaron thy brother, and his sons with him; and shalt anoint them, and consecrate them, and sanctify them, that they may minister unto me in the priest's office (Exodus 28:40-41 KJV).

And you shall take the anointing oil, pour it on his head, and anoint him (Exodus 29:7).

In the Exodus version of this same event, Moses uses the word "coat." In the Leviticus description, he changes "coat" to "garment." The coat is a prophetic parallel of the anointing that consecrates and separates us for the service of God.

When Israel configured the coat upon Joseph, it was much more than a father bestowing a gift upon a son. Israel was "mantling" Joseph with the anointing. As we prophetically parallel the coat of many colors, we incorporate three destiny dynamics of the anointing that will occur in your personal life.

The First Destiny Dynamic in the Anointing: You Will Participate in What is Prophetic

Prior to the coat of many colors being placed upon Joseph, there is no biblical evidence that he was a dreamer. However, the text is structured in context to present Joseph's dreams immediately after the conferring of the coat. One of the rules of biblical interpretation is context. This means the author's intent is known through the verses alone.

Understanding this hermeneutical principle there is no way we can escape the connecting components in the text between the coat as a type of anointing, and Joseph's dreams. Let's reexamine Genesis 37:3 and see how it is linked to the prophetic dreams that foretell Joseph's destiny in Egypt.

*Now Israel loved Joseph more than all his chil-
dren, because he was the son of his old age: and
he made him a coat of many colours. And when
his brethren saw that their father loved him
more than all his brethren, they hated him, and
could not speak peaceably unto him. And Joseph
dreamed a dream, and he told it his brethren: and they hated him yet the more* (Genesis
37:3-5 KJV).

What Joseph dreamed concerning the future was utterly
inconceivable—and it involved his brothers. You can imagine the envy and jealousy that already existed because Jacob
(Israel) showed such love toward Joseph, especially when he
was given the multicolored coat.

Now Joseph asked his brothers to gather around,
and he said:

*"Please hear this dream which I have dreamed:
There we were, binding sheaves in the field.
Then behold, my sheaf arose and also stood
upright; and indeed your sheaves stood all
around and bowed down to my sheaf." And his
brothers said to him, "Shall you indeed reign
over us? Or shall you indeed have dominion
over us?" So they hated him even more for his
dreams and for his words. Then he dreamed
still another dream and told it to his brothers, and said, "Look, I have dreamed another*

dream. And this time, the sun, the moon, and the eleven stars bowed down to me." So he told it to his father and his brothers; and his father rebuked him and said to him, "What is this dream that you have dreamed? Shall your mother and I and your brothers indeed come to bow down to the earth before you?" And his brothers envied him, but his father kept the matter in mind (Genesis 37:6-11).

The brothers were once again indignant, yet Joseph's father pondered the dream.

Who could have known these dreams foretold that Joseph would one day rule Egypt with Pharaoh's blessing and the famine-starved people in Canaan, including Joseph's own family, would come and humble themselves before him asking for food.

Beloved, Joseph the "dreamer" is a prophetic picture of what the prophet Joel promised (Joel 2:28-29) that was fulfilled on the day of Pentecost:

And it shall come to pass in the last days, says God, that I will pour out of My Spirit on all flesh; your sons and your daughters shall prophesy, your young men shall see visions, your old men shall dream dreams. And on My menservants and on My maidservants I will pour out My Spirit in those days; and they shall prophesy (Acts 2:17-18).

The sign of the coming of the Spirit in the last days will be that God would drench us in the anointing through dreams. Throughout Scripture, the text teaches that dreams from Heaven are a form of prophecy.

> *Then He said, "Hear now My words: If there is a prophet among you, **I, the Lord**, make Myself known to him in a vision; I **speak to him in a dream**"* (Numbers 12:6).

When leaving the land of Israel for Laban's house to flee from Esau, God appeared to Jacob in a dream to reconfirm and establish the blessing bestowed on him earlier by his father, Isaac (Genesis 28:10-17). Just as Jacob would confer the coat upon his son, Joseph, and as a result, he would "participate in the prophetic" through dreams, even so, did it also happen to Jacob years earlier.

Throughout Scripture, the text teaches that dreams from Heaven are a form of prophecy.

On the day Jacob went into his father's tent, the Bible says:

> *Then Rebekah took the choice clothes of her eldest son Esau, which were with her in the house, and put them on Jacob her younger son* (Genesis 27:15).

So he came to a certain place and stayed there all night, because the sun had set. And he took one of the stones of that place and put it at his head, and he lay down in that place to sleep. Then he dreamed, and behold, a ladder was set up on the earth, and its top reached to heaven; and there the angels of God were ascending and descending on it. ...Then Jacob rose early in the morning, and took the stone that he had put at his head, set it up as a pillar, and poured oil on top of it (Genesis 28:11-12,18).

Beloved, the oil Jacob poured on top of the stone he set for a pillar was a significant sign of the anointing.

I was invited to a series of charismatic groups for Holy Spirit seminars in Johannesburg, South Africa. My desperate desire since the 1980s was to go to South Africa and minister to the victims of the ruthless, unjust political system of apartheid. Upon receiving requests to minister, I realized the places that were designated for my ministry would not accomplish the intended purpose of traveling so far. I wanted to bring the anointing to those who had lost hope due to years of tears under the oppression that so violated their rights. I proceeded by faith forward onto the journey to arrange it, though I had no idea how.

The week I was about to leave, I had a dream that directed me into the destiny of God's plan. In it, I saw a huge hall packed with people of Indian descent. A Voice in the dream asked me the question, "Where are these people from?" I said, "Oh, Lord, these people are from India who live in Singapore." The Voice answered, "No, not from Singapore." Again, the voice asked me where the people were from. I answered in the same manner, "Oh, Lord, they are from India who live in Nairobi." The Voice continued to ask me the same question, as I answered the same from Malaysia and Bombay. The Voice said, "No, these are the people from Durban, South Africa."

I knew immediately from the night vision that even though I knew not a single soul there, I should inquire about charismatic groups in Durban when I arrived in Johannesburg. I followed the dream, knowing that it would direct me to exactly where the perfect will of God was, even though I would have to take an additional flight to get there.

Upon my arrival in South Africa, I made a diligent search, determined within myself, knowing God would help me get to the perfect place to fulfill the call. After probing and praying, the door opened to minister to the same people in the same auditorium I saw in my dream in Durban. It was a massive community of believers who were so hungry for the Holy Spirit. Hundreds received the baptism of the Spirit and spoke in tongues.

The Second Destiny Dynamic in the Anointing: The Perfection of Resurrection in Your Life.

Beloved, you may wonder why you had to go through so many unforeseen trials and tribulations for serving God. Did you ever ask, "God, why did You allow this? How could this happen to me?"

David says in Psalm 71:20-21:

> *You, who have shown me great and severe troubles, shall revive me again, and bring me up again from the depths of the earth. You shall increase my greatness, and comfort me on every side.*

In those verses of Scripture, David reveals how God will use our pain to train us for greatness.

In the Joseph narrative, the shredded, torn coat prophetically prefigures a devastated destiny. However, there is a *dunamis* dynamic in the anointing that foreshadows the perfection of resurrection in our lives.

Things that were dead come back to life when the anointing touches it. This can mean your body, a business, a relationship, your dream, or your vision. Whenever the anointing touches something, the perfection of resurrection is revealed.

In Genesis 37, Jacob was given the impression that Joseph was dead. After years of adversity Jacob finally returned to the land of his fathers, Abraham and Isaac. The sudden death of his beloved Rachel began a series of sorrows that the patriarch would endure in order to birth the nation that bore his spiritual name "Israel."

Little did Jacob know when he finally settled in the land of promise that new swells of storms were on the horizon.

Jacob knew the tension was beginning to boil between the son of his old age and his brothers, but how does an aged man handle the shock of being handed his youngest son's bloody coat? He was not aware when he sent Joseph on the journey to Shechem that he would never return to the tents so filled with memories of father and son.

On that dreadful day, in bewilderment, pressing his shaking hands upon the linen soaked with bloodstains into the tapestry so finely designed, he was forced to recognize it: *"And he recognized it and said, 'It is my son's tunic. A wild beast has devoured him. Without doubt Joseph is torn to pieces'"* (Genesis 37:33).

Beloved reader, maybe you were handed a "bloody and torn coat." Perhaps everything you worked for fell apart in a day. Maybe the dream came crashing down, and you thought you would never get it again, but we serve a God who can use our dilemma for destiny. The anointing will give you the strength to fully recover everything the enemy has stolen from your life.

In a personal prophetic sense of Scripture, Joseph's multicolored coat dipped in blood is a type and shadow of the blood of Christ. It proves the return of your loss through the power of the Cross. The blood foreshadows the price Jesus paid for you to rise out of the ruins of your past, into His prophetic promise. It reflects the perfection of the resurrection.

Just as Jesus rose from the dead, so will you rise into a place of power and victory.

Joseph's rise to power was of supernatural origin. The strong caste system, which was unbreakable for centuries in Egypt, was broken because of the anointing. A slave becomes second to Pharaoh.

Jacob never thought he would lay eyes upon Joseph again. The reunion of Jacob and Joseph was as if his son arose from the dead, foreshadowing the resurrection in our lives.

> *And Israel said to Joseph, "I had not thought to see your face; but in fact, God has also shown me your offspring!"* (Genesis 48:11).

The blood foreshadows the price Jesus paid for you to rise out of the ruins of your past, into His prophetic promise.

The Third Destiny Dynamic in the Anointing: The Anointing is God's Preservation Through all Your Desolation

Kathryn Kuhlman said, "Never, absolutely never give up. Never give in no matter what! Fight through! And I promise you with all my heart, God will help you."

Jesus told His disciples before He ascended into Heaven, *"You shall receive power when the Holy Spirit has come upon you..."* (Acts 1:8). My personal experience is that the anointing is the preserving power of God. No matter what tries to stop you, when the anointing is on your life, you will have the power to persevere.

You may ask, "What is the preserving power of the anointing?" The following Scriptures answer that question:

> *Now to Him who is able to keep you from stumbling, and to present you faultless before the presence of His glory with exceeding joy, to God our Savior, who alone is wise, be glory and majesty, dominion and power, both now and forever. Amen* (Jude 1:24-25).

> *Who are kept by the power of God through faith for salvation ready to be revealed in the last time* (1 Peter 1:5).

When I look back at the deepest, darkest days of my life, I know the reason I had the strength to stand and continue to press forward was because of the anointing. The anointing is a shield of preservation in our desolation.

> *Prepare the table, set a watchman in the tower, eat and drink. Arise, you princes, anoint the shield!* (Isaiah 21:5)

For Saul, in Second Samuel 1:21, the context conveys when he lost the anointing, he lost the shield:

The shield of the mighty is cast away there! The shield of Saul, not anointed with oil.

The anointing is a shield of preservation in our desolation.

One of the ways I learned to discover the secrets in God's Word was through directing my attention to details. Whenever I read the text and see something that appears to be irregular, I ask, "What does God want me to see by this obvious irregularity in the continuity and flow?"

Because all Scripture is inspired by God, and its origin infallible from the Holy Spirit, paying attention to details gives us the interpretation and revelation of the Author's objective. What appears to be seemingly insignificant can reveal God's greatest mysteries to us. Such is the case in Genesis 37:25. It is written in order to accentuate to us that the anointing would accompany Joseph into Egypt. Though his coat was taken from him, the anointing from the conferring of the coat stayed with him.

I believe Moses used minute details to demonstrate the preserving power of the anointing.

And they sat down to eat a meal. Then they lifted their eyes and looked, and there was a company of Ishmaelites, coming from Gilead with their camels, bearing spices, balm, and myrrh, on their way to carry them down to Egypt (Genesis 37:25).

In a hermeneutical sense of Scripture, the caravan carrying spices, balm, and myrrh are a direct connection to Exodus 30:23. In these passages, spices and myrrh are explicit expressions that also appear in the compound composite of the apothecary used to make the anointing oil of kinds, the tabernacle and furnishing the high priest of Israel. These similar expressions are a form of biblical hermeneutics called *gezerah shavah* in Hebrew. This means the divine design in Scripture connects the two because there are supernatural similarities.

The unusual format in Genesis 37:25 is due to the description of the items carrying Joseph down to Egypt. The way the text is written may seem irrelevant when Joseph has been traded into the hands of Ishmaelites for twenty pieces of silver. It seems insignificant to tell us on the caravan there was balm, spices, and myrrh. These vaguely apparent descriptions are in reality the source of power behind Joseph's survival and success in Egypt. They describe God's prescription of power in the anointing. They are carefully placed in the passage, so it becomes evident. The sale, the betrayal, and the difficult days in Egypt are the price behind the power that will be given to him.

Myrrh is the principal spice in the anointing not only because of fragrance but because of the cost. Myrrh in the ancient world was of a higher monetary value than pure gold.

This was the spice that Nicodemus used to anoint the body of Jesus in John 19:39:

> *And Nicodemus, who at first came to Jesus by night, also came, bringing a mixture of myrrh and aloes, about a hundred pounds.*

This commodity in the biblical era was used as a "preserving agent" for bodies when deceased. Likewise, myrrh is a preserving property in the anointing. This incredible correlation is a demonstration of how the preserving power of the anointing will keep us through every trial and tribulation in our lives.

> *Also take for yourself quality spices—five hundred shekels of liquid myrrh, half as much sweet-smelling cinnamon (two hundred and fifty shekels), two hundred and fifty shekels of sweet-smelling cane.... And you shall make from these a holy anointing oil, an ointment compounded according to the art of the perfumer. It shall be a holy anointing oil* (Exodus 30:23,25).

Do you desire the anointing and its preserving properties to enable you to remain faithful in the fire?

We are introduced to Joseph with test after test in Genesis chapters 37 through 40, but the tests are what qualified him for God's best. This is why the conferring of the coat and the anointing are the secrets behind his success.

Prayer for the Conferring of the Coat

Dear Holy Spirit,

Immerse me like the conferring of Joseph's coat. Let the anointing activate dreams and visions in my life. Use every disappointment, heartache, and sorrow as the price I am willing to pay for the anointing in my life. Amen.

Chapter 4

THE ANOINTING AND THE DIADEM OF DESTINY

Each young woman's turn came to go in to King Ahasuerus after she had completed twelve months' preparation, according to the regulations for the women, for thus were the days of their preparation apportioned: six months with oil of myrrh, and six months with perfumes and preparations for beautifying women.

—ESTHER 2:12

In order to live in this life, you need the comfort of the Holy Ghost.

–BISHOP GILBERT PATTERSON
(1939-2007), American Pentecostal
Leader, Church of God in Christ

AFTER READING ESTHER CHAPTER 2, HAVE YOU ever wondered how Esther achieved such an exalted state of position and power? Is it a proper assessment to think that Esther became queen because of beauty alone? Certainly, we know she was beautiful, but is the entire Jewish nation spared from Haman's diabolical demise because of her beauty?

Esther's role is going to require much more than something exterior. First, she needs to go through a proving process. As King Saul's ancestor, her unique calling will require that the legacy of the crown be restored by fulfilling what Saul forfeited. This will be done through completing the command given to Saul to destroy Amalek that he blatantly disobeyed.

In Exodus, God swore to His people *"that I will utterly blot out the remembrance of Amalek from under heaven"* (Exodus 17:14). This was because Amalek did not fear God and considered the miracle at the Red Sea as mere coincidence—denying God His glory. This was contrary to all the surrounding nations that understood it was the God of the Israelites who worked these mighty deeds.

Remember what Amalek did to you on the way as you were coming out of Egypt, how he met you on the way and attacked your rear ranks, all

*the stragglers at your rear, when you were tired
and weary; and he did not fear God. Therefore
it shall be, when the Lord your God has given
you rest from your enemies all around, in the
land which the Lord your God is giving you
to possess as an inheritance, that you will blot
out the remembrance of Amalek from under
heaven. You shall not forget* (Deuteronomy
25:17-19).

When the first king of Israel was anointed, his first
assignment given by God was to destroy Amalek so that God
might fulfill His word. Saul was chosen by God for this task
and received the anointing to accomplish this, but through
his rebellion and refusal to obey, Saul spared the king of the
Amalekites, King Agag. As a consequence of this deadly
decision, Agag's descendant Haman appears in the book of
Esther generations later. Haman is the evil engineer behind
the plan to utterly destroy the Jews.

During this time, Esther, Saul's descendant, will hero-
ically be the vessel God will use to reverse the curse. How
will she do this? It will be done through the anointing.

In this chapter, I want to teach you how the anointing works in our lives by using Queen Esther as a pattern
of power. I truly believe that as Esther was appointed and
anointed for *"such a time as this,"* so will you affect your generation because of the anointing.

Through the Anointing, You Will Become Drenched in Destiny

The oils mentioned in Esther 2 are supernaturally synonymous with the anointing. This comparison is carefully profiled by using specific words that appear in Esther 2:12 and Exodus 30:23. There are two specific words singled out in these verses that are connected in concept to one another.

...six months with oil of myrrh, and six months with perfumes... (Esther 2:12).

Also take for yourself quality spices—five hundred shekels of liquid myrrh, half as much sweet-smelling cinnamon (two hundred and fifty shekels), two hundred and fifty shekels of sweet-smelling cane.... This shall be a holy anointing oil to Me throughout your generations (Exodus 30:23,31).

The designated words used to describe the oils in Esther 2:12 are not to be viewed for outward purposes only. The comparison with Exodus 30 means they are to be understood in the context of the anointing because in those verses God commands Moses to make the anointing oil for kings and holy things in the tabernacle.

"Six months in oil of myrrh, and six months with perfumes" means that for twelve months, Esther was drenched for her destiny. The concept of the anointing is structured into the text as a prelude to Esther's platform. Immediately after being saturated, Esther becomes inaugurated into destiny.

The unusual favor given to her is directed and connected to the anointing. The doors are opened and she finds favor in the eyes of all who look upon her, which means she carried an attribute of favor given to her through the anointing.

> *...And Esther obtained **favor** in the sight of all who saw her* (Esther 2:15).

> *The king loved Esther more than all the other women, and she obtained grace and **favor** in his sight more than all the virgins; so he set the royal crown upon her head and made her queen instead of Vashti* (Esther 2:17).

If we make an observation, the idea of the anointing oil is proposed as a promise by which this astonishing favor is procured. The critical component of favor is a manifestation of the anointing that rests upon her.

The Anointing Accomplishes Transformation Beyond Our Limitation

I will never forget the first time I participated in a ministry of signs and wonders back in the 1970s. I was selected to be a "word of knowledge" worker with a renowned ministry of its day. Not everyone who was part of the ministry was permitted to engage in that special privilege. All I knew was that I wanted to be used of God in that capacity more than anything else in my life. I sought after the power of the Holy Spirit with all my being. I earnestly prayed before I was selected that my name would be called for such a mission.

Shortly after beseeching the Lord, the pastor assigned me to the post I desired, to work in "the word of knowledge" during the miracle services. My assignment was to walk softly and unseen up and down the aisles and identify healing by the Holy Spirit's leading.

One of these services was held in Escondido, California, in a church pastored by one of the great generals of the Charismatic Renewal, Harald Bredesen, who was a forerunner of the Charismatic Lutherans. The long-awaited moment had finally come to pass. As the music brought Heaven down, miracles began to be called out one by one through my pastor who was the guest speaker.

The adrenaline began to rush through my body as I slipped gently into the aisles to begin my search for those who had received healing. Much to my surprise, many people had faces like stone and seemed to resist what was happening.

As the healings continued to be announced, no one volunteered to say they were the ones with the particular illnesses and diseases that were being spoken of from the platform. The more I moved through the crowd, the more uncomfortable they seemed to be.

I began to struggle within myself. I did not know how to approach them. I began to panic because I had no natural way of knowing who was being healed. *Dear Lord,* I thought, *I never knew it would be so difficult.* Thoughts began to rush through my mind, *I could ruin the whole service if I can't find the persons who were the recipients of power.*

In my heart, I refused to go up to someone I was not sure about. The first five minutes felt like an eternity. Finally, I prayed again, "Holy Spirit, I can't do this of myself. I don't have the capacity in myself to see what You are doing, so I ask You to please open my eyes and show me who You are healing. I want to do this in an excellent way for the glory of God."

Immediately, He came through. It seemed as if the lights changed in the room. All of a sudden, a golden substance encircled certain individuals, but not all. I knew it was the glory resting on those who were healed. I stepped out in faith and carefully and gently asked one of the people with an expressionless demeanor, "Sir, I believe you are being healed." It was apparent to me that the Holy Spirit was helping me.

However, because many in the crowd seemed to be reserved, I wanted to be extra sensitive. Careful to say only what I felt He wanted me to say, I said again to the man, "If you move your leg, your healing will be complete." Then the man was touched and claimed his healing. What a few moments earlier was *pressure,* transformed into *power* because the Holy Spirit took over.

From that day forward, the supernatural manifestation of the Spirit of God never left my life. The work of the anointing is to enable us so that we know it is not us, but only Him working in us. Jesus told His disciples in John 14:17, *"He dwells with you and will be in you."* This means twenty-four hours a day we have access to His leading and prompting. Not just in spiritual matters but in every area of daily life. The

Holy Spirit will be more real to us than the breath we breathe when we learn to follow His anointing in everything.

One of the ways we clearly see how He takes us out of "limitation" to a place of "transformation" beyond our capacity is seen in the use of the name "Esther" versus "Esther the Queen." In Esther chapters 2 through 4, the text refers to her only as "Esther" except in one instance where she is referred to as "Esther the Queen."

"Isn't it the same?" you may ask, "What's the difference? She is both Esther and Esther the Queen." In the verses that display the summit of her predestined purpose, which is to destroy Amalek by bringing Haman the Agagite to downfall, the text uses "Esther the Queen."

In contrast, this title is not used in every reference where her name is mentioned. It is exclusively in the juncture in the text where the action that is being displayed contributes to Haman's destruction.

In Hebrew, the concept of kingship is *malchut*. *Malchut* is the expression of the furthest reach of one's highest destiny. When in the book of Esther she is referred to as "Esther the Queen," it is indicating she has come into the highest designated purpose of her life.

The Anointing Will Give You the Courage to be Dedicated unto Death

Doing the will of God is not always easy. Sometimes it is very demanding. We all face various opposition and obstacles we must overcome when striving to do God's will.

In 2014, I had planned a very important medical mission to Kenya. We were going to take thousands of dollars' worth of medication to people in great need. Everything was set in perfect order. Then suddenly, someone very dear to us unexpectedly passed away. It devastated us. It just so happened that the burial was scheduled the very same day as the clinic was to begin.

My heart was ripped in two. I knew the beloved Kenyan people had been expectedly waiting and planning our arrival for days, but I also felt an obligation to comfort those near to us who were affected by this tragedy. I knew in my heart—because of the size of the medical mission and unpredictable circumstances that can arise in customs when such a mission in the third world occurs—that my experience in such matters was needed in order for the clinic to be a success.

> What gave me the power to go forward and fulfill what God had called me to do amid such grievous and difficult circumstances? It was the anointing.

I recall crying and grieving in the night, asking God for the grace to make the decision I knew He wanted me to make for the sake of the poor in Kenya who were depending on me. It was to fulfill the mission that God entrusted me with no matter what the cost. In the morning, I was able by God's grace to complete the mission that led to many other missions and a great expansion of the work in Kenya. The following year, God provided wells of fresh water and feeding programs for the villages of Kenya we were privileged to serve.

When I look back, I see such an enlargement could not have taken place if I would have stayed behind the year before. What gave me the power to go forward and fulfill what God had called me to do amid such grievous and difficult circumstances? It was the anointing.

Yet my little experience cannot be measured to Esther's. In Esther 4, the Scripture brings out a similar struggle on a much greater magnitude. Esther is requested by her cousin Mordecai to go before the king and plead for her people. Esther, our model of great virtue and bravery, does not respond at first the way we expect. She has reservations and knows the political danger of barging into the king's throne room without an invitation. In the laws of the Medes and the Persians, such a breach of protocol was a death sentence unless the king stretched out his scepter to allow it. Esther's reluctant response is elevated by the decree established in Esther chapter 1 against women because of the former queen Vashti's behavior toward the king.

Esther's reaction to Mordecai is:

All the king's servants and the people of the king's provinces know that any man or woman

*who goes into the inner court to the king, who
has not been called, he has but one law: put all
to death, except the one to whom the king holds
out the golden scepter, that he may live. Yet I
myself have not been called to go in to the king
these thirty days* (Esther 4:11).

Esther was faced with the grave reality of death if she did
what was being required of her. Her choice to obey the voice
of God and risk her life for her people is an evident token of
the anointing and its power.

*Then Esther told them to reply to Morde-
cai: "Go, gather all the Jews who are present
in Shushan, and fast for me; neither eat nor
drink for three days, night or day. My maids
and I will fast likewise. And so I will go to the
king, which is against the law; and if I perish, I
perish!"* (Esther 4:15-16)

I am convinced that without enduring many trials, tribulations, and hardships required for the assignments God
has given me, that I could have never come forth in the level
of victory every time without the anointing.

Dedication unto death may not be only something
biological. It can also mean something that is a type of death-
to-self experience that the Holy Spirit needs so that the "life"
of Christ is revealed through you to others. *"Always carrying about in the body the dying of the Lord Jesus, that the life*

of Jesus also may be manifested in our body" (2 Corinthians 4:10).

In First Corinthians 15:31, the last line Paul says is, *"I die daily."* Dying daily is when the believer learns to put aside his or her own desires in order to put what the Spirit of God prefers above anything else. Doing this as a lifestyle requires a constant sensitivity toward always deffering to the leading of the Holy Spirit in everything. In Esther's case, the voice of the Holy Spirit and the revealed word of God came to her by very practical means.

Esther 2:10 tells us, *"Esther had not revealed her people or family, for Mordecai had charged her not to reveal it."*

To obey this commandment, even in Mordecai's absence behind the closed walls in the house of women, she deferred and preferred what he asked of her. Even after she rose to the role of Queen of Persia, this quality of humble submission and obedience characterized her life.

> *Now Esther had not revealed her family and her people, just as Mordecai had charged her, for Esther obeyed the command of Mordecai as when she was brought up by him* (Esther 2:20).

In a personal prophetic sense, Mordecai is a type of Holy Spirit or Voice of God. God's will is not always something we can easily know just because we are Christians. Esther's vocation to her people required that she concede to the command, not from her own will, but the will which had been revealed to her from above.

For if you remain completely silent at this time, relief and deliverance will arise for the Jews from another place, but you and your father's house will perish. Yet who knows whether you have come to the kingdom for such a time as this? (Esther 4:14)

Ouch! And thank You, Holy Spirit. If Esther had not been trained to put herself aside and die to what she was inclined to do, she would have never escalated or been elevated.

Prayer to Have the Courage to be Dedicated unto Death

Dear Holy Spirit,

I desire the diadem for the farthest reach of my highest destiny. Release the anointing of divine favor on my life. Extend me beyond my human capacity. I ask that this precious anointing gives me the power to always prefer and defer all I do into Your care and guidance. Amen.

Chapter 5

THE CONTAGIOUS COMPONENT OF THE ANOINTING

So he departed from there, and found Elisha the son of Shaphat, who was plowing with twelve yoke of oxen before him, and he was with the twelfth. Then Elijah passed by him and threw his mantle on him. And he left the oxen and ran after Elijah.

—1 Kings 19:19-20

The Pentecostal power, when you sum it up, is just more of God's love. If it does not bring more of God's love it's simply a counterfeit.

—APOSTLE WILLIAM JOSEPH
SEYMOUR (1870-1922), Father
of the Azusa Street Revival

ON THAT ORDINARY DAY, LITTLE DID ELISHA KNOW that by sunset his life would be changed forever. The encounter with the anointing so struck him that he left the oxen to serve Elijah until the day he was taken up.

Maybe you have had an experience with someone who so touched your life that even a brief moment with that person changed the course of your destiny. I believe there are divine appointments coordinated and orchestrated by Heaven. Just as Elijah passing by Elisha, the divinely arranged convergence impacted Elisha forever.

Let me describe how the contagious component in the anointing works. I was in Bombay, India, in January 1983. When I heard Mother Teresa was not in Calcutta but was Bombay, my heart leaped. I could hardly believe that the time for the special event would not interfere with my itinerary in the city. I was scheduled in the evening for a huge healing service, but somehow the timing was perfect.

Enduring the rickety ride, passing through the pungent odors of the slums made it seem that I was in another world. Babies were crying as mothers lowered them into the gutter water for their morning baths. After spotting the address, the van stopped in front of a house titled "Asha Daan." This place looked brighter compared to its surroundings. The atmosphere was filled with joy and expectation.

Hurriedly, I rushed into the courtyard of the house with the mixed clan who traveled with me. As "Strangers in the Night" by Frank Sinatra played over the loudspeakers in the courtyard, I marveled how God had arranged such perfect timing for such an intimate environment. There was so much love and hope in the atmosphere.

In she walked. Her white linen sari, lined with blue stripes and a cross pinned to the shoulder identified her. I became captivated by the presence of God that emulated from her. Dignitaries handed her a bouquet of flowers, and I watched, astounded, as she graciously placed them in the arms of a blind woman.

After the children performed their dances and speeches were made, tea and little cakes were served to everyone. Then she walked over to us. My eyes immediately fell to her worn sandals. The buckle had made a permanent imprint on her dry skin. Her toes were swollen from walking for miles, as she did daily when picking up the "throwaways" off the streets of Calcutta. Her kindness and personal interest in us overwhelmed me. She had the ability to make each person feel as if the only one in the room by speaking as if each of us had known her all our lives.

In that first encounter with Mother Teresa, I had no idea that the years ahead would be filled with so many "divine appointments" with her in the many countries to which I would travel. Even when she came to Los Angeles, I had no clue how I was invited to a small and private meeting in one of the houses she founded for the poor.

That was the day that transformed me for a greater level of destiny for which I was completely unprepared. Out of the blue I was told Mother Teresa would be in Los Angeles for a few hours and that I was invited to visit her on Edgeware Road. The tiny house was located in the Los Angeles housing projects. When I walked in, I tried to squeeze between the people. Somehow, one of the workers motioned me over to the only breathable space, which happened to be next to Mother Teresa.

As Mother was teaching her workers, I could not stop weeping and I felt so embarrassed. I was in the presence of pure love and humility standing next to her. I tried to hold back the tears, but the Holy Spirit was so present I could not contain myself. I knew Heaven was graciously imparting something I could feel in my body and soul that would affect my life forever.

DIVINE PROVIDENCE

What looks like a coincidence is actually divine providence. God prepares the passageway with supernatural setups for His plan in our lives. I had no inkling that those seemingly coincidental but truly providential meetings with Mother Teresa would inspire my steps and chart my course for future ministry. It seemed that every time I traveled to minister in a foreign country, Mother Teresa just "happened" to be there at the same time.

One of the greatest miracles I've ever witnessed came as a result of the moments with destiny I just described. In 2009,

I was scheduled to preach and hold a healing crusade at one of the largest charismatic groups in the Philippines. In years prior, we packed the Araneta Coliseum, which holds about 35,000 for such occasions. Just before the plane landed, the sunlight beamed like rays through the window next to me. Then I heard the Lord say, "I sent you here for one."

The voice of the Lord seemed to indicate that in order to "find" the one, I would need to be sensitive to His leading to search for the one He spoke of while fulfilling my many obligations in the country. I thought about it, yes, the multitudes were in His heart, but this mission was not about the throngs waiting—it was about one.

One the first night, the place was jammed; miracles happened everywhere throughout the auditorium as a result of the fiery faith and great anticipation of the people. When the meeting was over, I kept hearing the Lord's voice, "I sent you here for one." I determined at that moment to rise at 3 in the morning and go out to visit Tala. Tala was the location of Jose Rodrigues' hospital that housed lepers and those with incurable diseases. One of the hosts volunteered to take us on that long journey out to the place where I knew those stricken with Hansen's Disease lived.

That entire morning, I felt the longing of Jesus within me, searching for the one. As I passed through the corridors of the hospital, examining each patient, I did not feel the anointing. The kind nurse led us through every ward; although we gave gifts and prayed with the patients, I still did not witness within me that I had found the soul Jesus was looking for.

Tired and almost ready to leave, I asked the nurse, "Are these all the patients?" She replied, "There is one more ward, but it is all the way at the end." Lovingly, she guided us there.

Upon entering the room, there she was. A little girl reading a book. She had sores of leprosy all over her body and face. I wondered to myself how she could be so interested in reading in her condition. She was sitting at the edge of the bed, with her little legs hung over it. I gently approached her and said, "Hello sweetie, may I sit here?" She answered politely, "Yes, ma'am." "What's your name?" I asked her. She replied, "My name is Rosalee."

As we began to engage in conversation, the anointing began to fall. By this, I knew she was the soul Jesus had sent me to find among the thousands. After conversing with her for a few minutes, I introduced those with me and asked her, "Sweetie, would you mind if I put you on my lap for a few minutes?" She said, "Yes ma'am."

I lifted her tiny body that felt like only skin and bones and began to pray over her and rock her in my arms. Jesus' love for her was burning inside me. Later I found out she was an orphan, and because of her leprosy, she had been abandoned by her brothers and sisters after her mother died.

The time came when I had to leave. Before I left, I put little sticky notes under her pillow, on her book, and everywhere I could think of that said, "Jesus loves you and Auntie Michelle loves you."

I felt so torn upon leaving, but somehow knew I would see her again. In order not to leave undone the assignment that the Lord had given me, I asked a local man of God if he and his family would look after her and send me reports. Within two weeks I received the news that she was completely healed and no longer a patient in the leprosy ward. Today, she is part of my ministry staff in the Philippines. She went on to receive a degree in teaching and is happily married. She remains one of the most powerful prayer warriors I know.

Consequently, it was clear to me that the encounters with Mother Teresa all around the world resulted in something being deposited into my life. I would have been unable to sense His search and thirst for one soul if those destiny-designed moments with her did not happen. That experience, way back on Edgeware Road, facilitated the contagious component in the anointing.

Similarly, as described in my personal experience, the Bible teaches there are contagious components in the anointing. These components or properties can affect us through individuals, or powerful encounters where the anointing is present.

This can also happen through the laying on of hands when a man or woman of God (who is truly proven to be one of God's generals) "imparts" the anointing to us. Second

Timothy 1:6 says, *"Therefore I remind you to stir up the gift of God which is in you through the laying on of my hands."*

HOW THE CONTAGIOUS COMPONENT WORKS

For the rest of this chapter, I want to teach you from God's word how the contagious component in the anointing works.

On the day of Saul's anointing, the prophet Samuel directed the first king of Israel to go on a journey. This excursion was for the purpose of imparting the *prophetic* attributes to the anointing he already received.

Samuel intended to secure this important role as king with an ability to prophetically govern Israel with wisdom and knowledge not of this world. These prophetic attributes were also needed for battle when Israel would engage in warfare with enemies of God.

In First Samuel 10, immediately after Saul is anointed by Samuel, he is directed by him to join himself to a company of prophets: *"Then Samuel took a flask of oil and poured it on his head, and kissed him and said: "Is it not because the Lord has anointed you commander over His inheritance?"* (1 Samuel 10:1).

Through prophecy, Samuel gave Saul details concerning where the company of prophets would be located and how Saul was to join himself to them. Scripture expands upon exactly what the prophets were wearing and what they would be doing when Saul found them (1 Samuel 10:3-13).

When initially reading these verses, the question I always asked myself was, "Why is Scripture elaborating in these particulars concerning the prophets, and why is Samuel so insistent on Saul joining them while they were prophesying?"

After understanding the secret of the contagious component in the anointing, I finally grasped what the text was enunciating in that passage. Samuel wanted Saul's anointing to be drenched with prophetic properties. As king, he would need levels of prophecy to guide the nation in the form of wisdom and understanding, which, when given by God, are prophetic in nature.

When Saul joined the company of prophets, the same prophetic spirit that was upon them came upon him.

After that you shall come to the hill of God where the Philistine garrison is. And it will happen, when you have come there to the city, that you will meet a group of prophets coming down from the high place with a stringed instrument, a tambourine, a flute, and a harp before them; and they will be prophesying. Then the Spirit of the Lord will come upon you, and you will prophesy with them and be turned into another man. ...When they came there to the hill, there was a group of prophets to meet him; then the Spirit of God came upon him, and he prophesied among them. ...Then a man from there answered and said, "But who is their father?"

Therefore it became a proverb: "Is Saul also among the prophets?" (1 Samuel 10:5-6,10,12).

> ## Samuel wanted Saul's anointing to be drenched with prophetic properties.

Have you ever asked yourself how the twelve were sent forth to preach, heal, and cast out demonic spirits before they were baptized in the Spirit? In Acts 1:8 (KJV), Scripture is clear that after the coming of the Spirit on the day of Pentecost, supernatural signs and wonders would follow. We know that after the day of Pentecost, the 120 were baptized in the Holy Spirit and Acts 1:8 became a reality.

Before ascending into Heaven, Jesus gave His final instruction to His Church: *"John truly baptized with water, but you shall be baptized with the Holy Spirit not many days from now"* (Acts 1:5).

We know these miraculous acts were a result of the baptism in the Spirit, but how do we reconcile the twelve being used of God in these supernatural signs *before* the resurrection and before the Spirit was given on the day of Pentecost?

> *And He* [Jesus] *called the twelve to Himself, and began to send them out two by two, and gave them power over unclean spirits* (Mark 6:7).

More specifically in Luke 10, Jesus sent forth the seventy and gave them instruction to heal the sick, yet the day of Pentecost had not yet taken place.

> *After these things the Lord appointed seventy others also, and sent them two by two before His face into every city and place where He Himself was about to go. ...And heal the sick there, and say to them, "The kingdom of God has come near to you"* (Luke 10:1,9).

We can reconcile these Scriptures through understanding the contagious component in the anointing. In a hermeneutical sense of Scripture, the key word in the verses cited is *"seventy."* As mentioned previously, certain words and phrases that are similar expressions are also found in other passages and are related to one another.

If we cite a passage that we know is like that in another place, it means the similarities are significant to the meaning. In Hebrew, this methodology is called *gezerah shavah.*

> *So the Lord said to Moses: "Gather to Me seventy men of the elders of Israel, whom you know to be the elders of the people and officers over them; bring them to the tabernacle of meeting, that they may stand there with you. Then I will come down and talk with you there. I will take of the Spirit that is upon you and will put the same upon them; and they shall bear the burden of the people with you, that you may not*

bear it yourself alone." ...Then the Lord came down in the cloud, and spoke to him, and took of the Spirit that was upon him, and placed the same upon the seventy elders; and it happened, when the Spirit rested upon them, that they prophesied, although they never did so again (Numbers 11:16-17,25).

This astounding wonder that occurred in the wilderness foreshadows Jesus sending forth the seventy before they were baptized in the Spirit. It was through being under the mantle of Jesus' anointing that they also became anointed. They ate with Him. They served with Him. They were personally trained by Him. By being near Him all the time, they were affected by the anointing on Jesus—with His word He could send them forth on the same mission with His authority guiding them.

The anointing upon Jesus affected His twelve disciples in such a way that His messianic mantle of healing, casting out devils, and deliverance also came upon them to be an extension of His work as prefigured with Moses in the desert and the seventy elders.

There is no way the twelve could escape the anointing after being near the Anointed One of Israel. I can imagine after being in the open-air meetings of bread multiplying, the blind seeing, the deaf hearing, and devils bowing that the power and contagious component from being with Him would also affect them.

This concept is prefigured in the unique relationship between Moses and Joshua. Throughout Scripture, the text teaches that mantles were given as a form of spiritual inheritance:

> *And the Lord said to Moses: "Take Joshua the son of Nun with you, a man in whom is the Spirit, and lay your hand on him.... And you shall give some of your authority to him, that all the congregation of the children of Israel may be obedient"* (Numbers 27:18,20).

For instance, Joshua was chosen to take Israel to the next level of destiny. He became the spiritual successor of Moses. Scripture goes out of its way to demonstrate the reason why Joshua was elected and selected for such a task.

Joshua was particularly close to Moses and had the privilege and responsibility of being his attendant for forty years. Joshua is referred to as "Moses' servant." This job description allowed him to be close to Moses, which would be necessary for his own destiny to bring Israel into the Promised Land. Because Joshua's future destiny required an anointing, he was not only trained, but also contagious components were imparted to him.

You may ask, "Does the term 'Moses' servant' only mean attendant?"

As a result of forty years of serving under the anointing Moses was carrying, Joshua was chosen to be his spiritual successor. However, Scripture indicates that there were certain attitudes of the heart and spiritual demeanor that especially qualified Joshua for such a task. The biblical record accentuates a caliber of character in him like no other.

These traits appear in a juncture of the text where Joshua's loyalty and faithfulness is exceptional. In the midst of crisis, difficulty, and division Joshua always emerges the same. He is proven in motives and actions to be a true servant. These junctures converge with actions that display unsurpassed loyalty and oneness in Spirit to the vision and leadership given to Moses by God. In particular, when there was dissension with the spies who returned with an evil report from the land of Canaan, Joshua rallied consistently in vision.

> But Joshua the son of Nun and Caleb the son of Jephunneh, who were among those who had spied out the land, tore their clothes; and they spoke to all the congregation of the children of Israel, saying: "The land we passed through to spy out is an exceedingly good land. If the Lord delights in us, then He will bring us into this land and give it to us, 'a land which flows with milk and honey.' Only do not rebel against the Lord, nor fear the people of the land, for they are our bread; their protection has departed from them, and the Lord is with us. Do not fear them" (Number 14:6-9).

Such nobility of character became the credentials Scripture requires to be a spiritual successor. Joshua also persevered in prayer for Moses, the man of God.

So the Lord spoke to Moses face to face, as a man speaks to his friend. And he would return to the camp, but his servant Joshua the son of Nun, a young man, did not depart from the tabernacle (Exodus 33:11).

So Moses arose with his assistant Joshua, and Moses went up to the mountain of God (Exodus 24:13).

When Moses ascended the mount for forty days and forty nights, Joshua was not disconnected from what was happening, even though Moses went up to the mountain. He remained faithful in prayer, one in the Spirit, supporting faithfully all God was doing in Moses. Therefore, the mantle came upon Joshua as a result of never doing his own thing. He was like the sons of Korah in Numbers 16 with singleness of heart, faithfully performing his God-given assignment.

Friend, in this chapter we have learned that the anointing is transmittable. It can transform us when we become connected to someone or come under an atmosphere where the anointing is present.

Let's ask ourselves: Have I recognized the divine encounters God has arranged with individuals He has ordained to change my life forever? Can I make the decision to be loyal and unswerving in my commitment, like Joshua? Am I convinced that if I stay close, under the cover and committed to the anointing that what God did then He will graciously do again in me?

The anointing is transmittable. It can transform us when we become connected to someone or come under an atmosphere where the anointing is present.

Prayer to Claim the Contagious Component of the Anointing

Dear Holy Spirit,

I give You permission to guide me into the place where Your anointing is flowing. I ask You to grant me the experience of the seventy who were sent by Jesus in Matthew 10. I claim divine encounters with men and women You have ordained to change my life forever. Amen.

Chapter 6

THE ANOINTING AND YOUR MIRACULOUS MOMENT

But you shall receive power when the Holy Spirit has come upon you; and you shall be witnesses to Me in Jerusalem, and in all Judea and Samaria, and to the end of the earth.

—ACTS 1:8

"Then I asked God to give me the power He gave the Galilean fishermen—to anoint me for service."
—MARIA WOODWORTH ETTER (1844-1924),
American Pentecostal Pioneer, Author
of *A Diary of Signs and Wonders*

ACHIEVING THE FARTHEST REACH
OF YOUR HIGHEST DESTINY

The anointing is God's tool to make you His masterpiece. Every facet of your life is a skilled work of art in the hand of the Master Designer.

> *For we are His workmanship, created in Christ Jesus for good works, which God prepared beforehand that we should walk in them* (Ephesians 2:10).

Within the design of that work, there is one miraculous moment distinct from all others. The time I am referring to varies in each destiny. For one person it may be a year within the tapestry of His plan. For another, it may be certain years of your life that sum up the mission statement of your life's highest calling.

In this chapter, I want to teach you about the incredible collision between time and destiny.

The most astounding instances in the Bible where this occurs is at the anointing at Bethany, six days before Jesus accomplished His highest destiny on earth, which was Calvary's Cross.

In order to evaluate this important work of the anointing in Jesus that is available to us, let's glance at the meaning of

His mission as the anointed of God. First, as mentioned previously, as the Messiah, His identity is the anointed of God.

> *How God anointed Jesus of Nazareth with the*
> *Holy Spirit and with power, who went about*
> *doing good and healing all who were oppressed of*
> *the devil, for God was with Him* (Acts 10:38).

There is no other who ever lived among us anointed like Jesus. There is no other in God's Word who unveils the anointing like Him. He possesses the seven attributes of the anointing foretold by Isaiah. (In the Bible, the number 7 is a symbol of perfection.)

> *The Spirit of the Lord shall rest upon Him, the*
> *Spirit of wisdom and understanding, the Spirit*
> *of counsel and might, the Spirit of knowledge*
> *and of the fear of the Lord* (Isaiah 11:2).

Jesus had a unique, one-of-a-kind relationship with the Holy Spirit above all others before Him. Now through His death and resurrection, you can participate in the promises of the Father. Jesus said: *"...but to wait for the Promise of the Father, 'which,' He said, 'you have heard from Me; for John truly baptized with water, but you shall be baptized with the Holy Spirit not many days from now'"* (Acts 1:4-5).

This holy bond between Jesus and the Holy Spirit can only be understood in the light of proper Christology. Christology is a theological term for the study of Jesus Christ that primarily concerns itself with the two natures of Christ, being true God and true man.

As true God, not in any way inferior to the Father, He is preexistent: *"In the beginning was the Word, and the Word was with God, and the Word was God"* (John 1:1). As true man, He is fully man with a true DNA link to the line of David: *"And the Word became flesh and dwelt among us, and we beheld His glory, the glory as of the only begotten of the Father, full of grace and truth"* (John 1:14).

These two natures subsist in perfection in the person of Jesus Christ and are foretold in Isaiah 9:6: *"For unto us a Child is born, unto us a Son is given; and the government will be upon His shoulder. And His name will be called Wonderful, Counselor, Mighty God, Everlasting Father, Prince of Peace."*

To clarify, in Jesus' nature as man, for the sake of our salvation He completely relied on the Holy Spirit for all of His works. Furthermore, Isaiah prophesied this dependence on the Holy Spirit by the Messiah in Isaiah 61:1:

> *The Spirit of the Lord God is upon me, because the Lord has anointed Me to preach good tidings to the poor; He has sent Me to heal the broken- hearted, to proclaim liberty to the captives, and the opening of the prison to those who are bound.*

Now that we have explored why Jesus as man, for the purpose of redeeming humankind, relied on the Holy Spirit, I want to take you back in Scripture to His anoint- ing at Bethany: *"Then Mary took a pound of very costly oil of spikenard, anointed the feet of Jesus, and wiped His feet with her hair. And the house was filled with the fragrance of the oil"* (John 12:3).

Let's look at the concepts of *inauguration* and *implementation* that are significant aspects of the anointing.

Inauguration: The Anointing will Inaugurate and Consecrate You for Your Miraculous Moment with Destiny

The first property of power explained is *inauguration*. Let's go back to the first century, just six days before Passover in the town of Bethany.

An indication of danger presented itself as they journeyed toward Jerusalem. The turmoil arose in their hearts as the twelve made their Passover pilgrimage. Every step into the Holy City in the past became a countdown to that final entry.

Calvary weighed heavily upon Jesus. In love, He trod this perilous path and arrived in Bethany. Footsteps upon the crackling rocks announced His arrival. The conversing voices in the distance caused her heart to leap. The Master was nigh. Sensing the familiar presence of mercy and kindness, she reverently met her guests at the door.

It was six days before the feast. Throngs embarked upon their pilgrimage to go up to Jerusalem. Soon the pungent smell of lamb's blood would permeate the city. Jesus had been on His way amid the multitudes. His journey to the Holy City concluded in Bethany. His close companions, Martha,

Mary, and Lazarus, affectionately anticipated His customary meal with them.

As He sat at the table with them, Mary did the unthinkable. She broke the alabaster box filled with the costly ointment of spikenard and began to anoint the feet of Jesus.

Then Mary took a pound of very costly oil of spikenard, anointed the feet of Jesus, and wiped His feet with her hair. And the house was filled with the fragrance of the oil (John 12:3).

When examining this Scripture, a significant addition to the anointing at Bethany is elaborated upon by Mark. His version says, *"...she poured it on* [anointed] *His head"* (Mark 14:3). In a literal sense, both versions complete themselves. Each one combined emphasizes an anointing from head to toe. The anointing on the feet of Jesus, as recorded by John, represent feet that would be nailed to a cross. The oil that poured forth as stated in Mark foretells of the crowning with thorns.

Mary was entirely unaware of the monumental significance the anointing would have on His passion and burial: *"But Jesus said, "Let her alone; she has kept this for the day of My burial"* (John 12:7).

In a contextual sense of Scripture, the anointing at Bethany should be assessed through the emphasis the apostle makes on time. This demonstrates the power property of inauguration in the anointing. John employs a unique literary tool that distinctly separates Jesus' three years of ministry from His last week on earth. This is a consecration in time. The apostle John separates time frames between Jesus' words in John 2:4, *"Woman, what does your concern have to do with Me? My hour has not yet come,"* in clear contrast to, My hour has come.

This trend is not just about the beginning of miracles. However, *"My time is not yet come"* continues throughout His three years of ministry. In another place, Jesus says, *"My time has not yet come, but your time is always ready"* (John 7:6).

The third demonstration of this is in John 7:8, *"...for My time has not yet fully come."*

The fourth instance is in John 8:20, *"...for His hour had not yet come."*

This repetition is designed to clearly contrast when He finally declares, *"the hour has come."* This precipitated pattern demonstrates the long-awaited hour Jesus was destined for. It cannot be compared to any other time in His life on earth because it is the reason He was sent.

Therefore John uses the anointing in Bethany to transition Him into this foreordained moment. If we follow closely in the context, methodically, it was immediately after Mary anointed Him that Jesus declares, *"the hour has come."* Therefore, the anointing is linked to that transition in time. If we continue in the context of John 12:3, the text portrays a transitioning element through the apparent time referring to the hour has come.

But Jesus answered them, saying, "The hour has come that the Son of Man should be glorified" (John 12:23).

Consistently and insistently the gospels connect all of the junctures of His hour that has finally come, only with the last week of His life on earth.

Let's verify this evidence. At the Last Supper, the narrative begins with *"...when Jesus knew His hour had come..."* (John 13:1) and also at the Garden of Gethsemane, *"Father, the hour has come"* (John 17:1). I believe just as the anointing transitioned Jesus into His time, so shall it for you.

Just as Mary anointed Jesus and afterward the text transitions time, so does the anointing propel you into your predestined purpose.

Implementation: The Decision to Do God's Will

Have you ever thought to yourself, *Why is God allowing this to happen to me if I am in His will?* And have you ever said the words, "I don't know if I can survive this. How can I do God's will when facing so many obstacles and attacks?"

For some of us, the trials we've been handed in life can be unimaginably shocking. One thing is sure, Jesus said, *"...In the world you will have tribulation; but be of good cheer; I have overcome the world"* (John 16:33).

We can get confused about the tests that come to try us before God opens the doors of opportunity He promised us. Oftentimes, the enemy of our soul can take advantage of us in difficult times and deceive us out of our destinies by enticing us to give up. Remember, it is possible to press past every circumstance assigned to stop you. You can receive the power to serve God and do His will no matter what diabolical plot tries to stop you. Yes, there may be struggles, but the anointing enables you to conquer and complete your heavenly assignment.

This is demonstrated in the words of the Savior, *"Father, if it is Your will, take this cup away from Me; nevertheless not My will, but Yours be done"* (Luke 22:42).

Jesus in the Garden is an archetype of how the power property of implementation works. In a systematic sense of Scripture, the Garden of Olives trails just after the anointing at Bethany. After Jesus' entrance into Jerusalem and His last Passover meal with the twelve, He departed for Gethsemane.

This garden was not like the "first" garden where the "first Adam" disobeyed God's will. The Garden of Gethsemane is where the "second Adam"—Jesus Christ—vanquished all powers of darkness and sin through His obedience unto death.

The property of implementation to do God's will is prophetically paralleled in three supernatural steps. These steps are taken from Matthew 26:36-55 on the night of His arrest in Gethsemane.

The Hebrew translation of the word "Gethsemane" is "oil press." Literally, this was a place of pressing out the oil. The spiritual significance of this name mirrors correspondent truths about how "fresh oil" exudes in our lives. Scripture marks these in a methodical order.

You can receive the power to serve God and do His will no matter what.

1.   The Supernatural Stretch into Another Place: "He went a little farther..." (Matthew 26:39).

These words begin the Gethsemane experience. They illustrate not only a geographical difference in physical location, but they reveal in a deeper sense how Jesus stretched beyond His human capabilities through this place of the oil press.

Allow me to take you there for a moment. The sorrows of sin began to grip His soul. It is imperative to remember He was fully aware of each step ahead of Him. In every stage He gave consent. For example, He released Judas to betray Him: *"...Then said Jesus to him, "What you do, do quickly"* (John 13:27). No man took Jesus' life, He gave it freely.

Shadows swiftly shut out the brilliance of the moon as Jesus began His travail. Unbearable grief began to seize Him. The stillness was eerie. Faraway sounds of creatures in the night seemed to scream impending danger. Jesus could have chosen differently; instead of calling 10,000 angels overlooking from Heaven, *He went a little farther.*

The same power that forged Him ahead is the same power available to you in the anointing.

2. **Selfless Service unto Him: "...nevertheless, not as I will, but as You will" (Matthew 26:39).**

The second supernatural step gives *explanation to the implementation* of choosing God's will over our own. Sometimes that process is challenging. Other times, to do what He wants seems unattainable. It is not a sin to battle and agonize over doing God's will. It only becomes sin when we refuse it. The anointing strengthens us not only to accomplish it, but to overcome ungodly resistance preventing us to perform it.

3. **Evidence of the Precedence of Love Working in You: "Friend, why have you come?" (Matthew 26:50).**

The anointing is like a secret weapon that will enable us to master our emotions. *"Rise, let us be going. See, My betrayer is at hand"* (Matthew 26:46). Jesus knew His betrayer was close. He was fully aware of what had been schemed in that treacherous kiss. Yet, Matthew tells us of the meekness in which He mastered His emotions by calling Judas *"friend."*

One of the greatest supernatural signs of the anointing is the wonder of loving one's enemies. To love our enemies is not possible if the only capacity to love another is with human love. This miracle depends on love that is not of this world. Jesus said in Matthew 7:20, *"Therefore by their fruits you will know them."*

Some giants we face are not physical. They can be emotional within ourselves or spiritual.

The enemy prevailing in the Garden was seeking a way for Jesus not to accomplish His task at the Cross. If Jesus would have demonstrated even a tinge of emotion originating from anger, bitterness, or revenge, it could have interfered with His mission. He who knew no sin became sin for us.

For He made Him who knew no sin to be sin for us, that we might become the righteousness of God in Him (2 Corinthians 5:21).

Like our Lord, we too can draw upon the anointing to walk in love.

As a champion, Jesus mastered every emotion. The anointing gave Him the power to exhibit love to Judas in the battle against all the principalities of darkness.

Like our Lord, we too can draw upon the anointing to walk in love with mastered emotions at all times. The Holy Spirit gives us the strength to vanquish any strife, anger, bitterness, revenge, evil speaking, evil imagination toward others, and any works of the flesh.

For those who live according to the flesh set their minds on the things of the flesh, but those who live according to the Spirit, the things of the Spirit. For to be carnally minded is death, but to be spiritually minded is life and peace. Because

*the carnal mind is enmity against God; for it is
not subject to the law of God, nor indeed can be.
So then, those who are in the flesh cannot please
God* (Romans 8:5-8).

Unmastered emotions can grieve the Holy Spirit and
interfere with the flow of the anointing: *"Do not grieve the
Holy Spirit of God, by whom you were sealed for the day of
redemption"* (Ephesians 4:30).

David's response to Saul exemplifies how the anointing
gives us the *power to master emotions.* King David, as God's
anointed, encapsulates how the anointing will give you the
power to master emotions.

*Then Abishai said to David, "God has deliv-
ered your enemy into your hand this day. Now
therefore, please, let me strike him at once with
the spear, right to the earth; and I will not have
to strike him a second time!" But David said
to Abishai, "Do not destroy him; for who can
stretch out his hand against the Lord's anointed,
and be guiltless?" David said furthermore, "As
the Lord lives, the Lord shall strike him, or his
day shall come to die, or he shall go out to battle
and perish* (1 Samuel 26:8-10).

These texts display a mastering of emotions evidenced
in David's life of constant prayer and increased anointing.
First Samuel 26:1-25 is actually the final test before David
possessed God's promise of becoming king. If we examine

Scripture closely, this test is actually a second version of a previous test that he did not pass perfectly.

The first one was in First Samuel 24. The settings were almost identical, differing only in one point. In First Samuel 24, the narrative acts as its own commentary and tell us, *"Now it happened afterward that David's heart troubled him because he had cut Saul's robe"* (1 Samuel 24:5).

Cutting off a piece of Saul's robe when he had the power to kill Saul seems completely minuscule and minor. However, for David it was not irrelevant. His entire destiny depended upon the years of testing with Saul. The tests were a source of spiritual analysis that proved there was no anger, revenge, bitterness, or resentment toward Saul.

Psalm 39:1-3 presents the proof of David's struggle and complete trust in God not to sin in his emotions toward Saul:

> *I said, "I will guard my ways, lest I sin with my tongue; I will restrain my mouth with a muzzle, while the wicked are before me." I was mute with silence, I held my peace even from good; and my sorrow was stirred up. My heart was hot within me; while I was musing, the fire burned. Then I spoke with my tongue* (Psalm 39:1-3).

Beloved, let us claim every property of power available in the anointing. Let us ask the Holy Spirit to help us be willing to be pressed to do God's will. That He would stretch us out farther to do the exploits, and that He would give us power through the anointing to master every emotion so we may reach the expected end—our God-determined destinies.

Prayer to Possess the Properties of Power

> *Dear Holy Spirit,*
>
> *I claim that the power properties in the anointing will inaugurate me for the time appointed. I also ask for the power property of implementation to do the will of my heavenly Father at any cost. Teach me how to go farther. I want to say, "Not my will but Thine be done." I declare that my emotions will be under Your subjection. Reveal anything that is not like Jesus in me. I am believing for personal outpouring greater than I can ask or think. Amen.*

Chapter 7

THE ANOINTING AND THE ROLE OF THE HOLY SPIRIT

And I will pray the Father, and He will give you another Helper [Comforter], that He may abide with you forever.

—John 14:16

"What is my task? First of all, my task is to be pleasing to Christ. To be empty of self and be filled with Himself. To be filled with the Holy Spirit; to be led by the Holy Spirit."
—AIMEE SEMPLE MCPHERSON (1890-1944),
Pentecostal Evangelist, Founder
of the International Church of
the Foursquare Gospel

I T ALL BEGINS WITH YOUR RELATIONSHIP WITH THE
Holy Spirit. He is the only One who will make Jesus alive
and personal to you every minute of your life. Jesus said:

> *However, when He, the Spirit of truth, has*
> *come, He will guide you into all truth; for He*
> *will not speak on His own authority, but what-*
> *ever He hears He will speak; and He will tell*
> *you things to come. He will glorify Me, for He*
> *will take of what is Mine and declare it to you*
> (John 16:13-14).

Because of this reality that Jesus revealed, our commu-
nion with Him is critical. During His last hours on earth,
He made provision that you and I would never be left alone
without the consolation of hearing His voice and feeling His
presence. Jesus said:

> *These things I have spoken to you while being*
> *present with you. But the Helper* [Comforter],
> *the Holy Spirit, whom the Father will send in*
> *My name, He will teach you all things, and*
> *bring to your remembrance all things that I said*
> *to you* (John 14:25-26).

Jesus wanted us—who never witnessed His glory in the
flesh—to be able to experience His loving presence as much

or even more than when He walked on this earth for thirty-three years. He never intended to leave us without having continual fellowship with Him at all times.

In your time of need, He wants you to sense and feel His nearness, as He did when He stretched out His hands in compassion to heal the sick, cleanse the lepers, and raise the dead. He provides the same power to heal, deliver, set free, and work miracles today as He did 2,000 years ago. Jesus said:

> *These things I have spoken to you, that in Me you may have peace. In the world you will have tribulation; but be of good cheer, I have overcome the world* (John 16:33).

How does He do this? Through the Holy Spirit. He is the only One who can fully reveal Jesus and make Him alive to you. He will only speak what Jesus is saying and only do what Jesus is doing. He will bring everything Jesus does and all Jesus says and manifest it to you. When you need direction, He wants to speak it to you. If you are in question concerning what your purpose on earth is, He is available to you.

On the night of Jesus' last supper, His heart was heavy and overflowing with love. His concern was not for Himself but His own: *"I pray for them. I do not pray for the world but for those whom You have given Me, for they are Yours"* (John 17:9). At that dinner, His burden was not for His sufferings that lay ahead. In His tenderness, each of the disciples He loved to the end:

Now before the Feast of the Passover, when Jesus knew that His hour had come that He should depart from this world to the Father, having loved His own who were in the world, He loved them to the end (John 13:1).

His love was so fervent even though knowing they would forsake Him and that even Peter would deny Him—yet He would continue to love them through it all.

The stillness ruled over the night. The burning torches propped up on the stone walls flickered. Eyes of mercy permeated to the core. Each one would have a significant role that was necessary for the hour. For this reason, as tender as a shepherd, Jesus made provision to comfort them because He was going away.

Leaving the twelve to return to His Father was part of the necessary plan. No matter what their weakness, He chose them. He loved them, and His first concern was for them. This is why at that hour Jesus told them He would send them another Comforter, a Helper, who would remove the emptiness of Jesus' absence. The Holy Spirit's mission was to make Jesus alive in their midst again—and He does the same for us today.

Nevertheless I tell you the truth. It is to your advantage that I go away; for if I do not go away, the Helper [Comforter] *will not come to you; but if I depart, I will send Him to you* (John 16:7).

The Holy Spirit is the Promise of the Father, the One Jesus sent so that through Him you will always experience help and comfort:

> But the Helper, the Holy Spirit, whom the Father will send in My name, He will teach you all things, and bring to your remembrance all things that I said to you (John 14:26).

Beloved in this chapter I direct your attention to *two power points* that enable you to have a *supernaturally sensitive* walk with the Holy Spirit. My objective is that your relationship with Him will be transformed by learning to lean on Him for everything.

Your relationship with Him will be transformed by learning to lean on Him for everything.

1. *The Holy Spirit Is a Person, Not Just a Power*

Jesus presents the Holy Spirit as a person through the use of personal pronouns. He chose this as a prelude to His passion because the era of the Holy Spirit was to begin fifty days after His resurrection. The Holy Spirit's initial presence on earth was in the Upper Room and continues until Jesus returns for His Church.

And it shall come to pass in the last days, says God, that I will pour out of My Spirit on all flesh; your sons and your daughters shall prophesy, your young men shall see visions, your old men shall dream dreams. And on My menservants and on My maidservants I will pour out My Spirit in those days; and they shall prophesy. I will show wonders in heaven above and signs in the earth beneath: blood and fire and vapor of smoke. The sun shall be turned into darkness, and the moon into blood, before the coming of the great and awesome day of the Lord (Acts 2:17-20).

While introducing the Holy Spirit at the Last Supper, Jesus continually refers to Him with personal pronouns such as "He, Him, and Himself." In particular, these references are exhibited throughout the book of John, chapters 14–16. The text accentuates the Holy Spirit as a person:

*The Spirit of truth whom the world cannot receive, because it neither sees **Him** nor knows **Him**; but you know **Him**, for **He** dwells with you and will be in you* (John 14:17).

2. Attributes of the Holy Spirit as a Person

The Holy Spirit is the Spirit of Truth

One of the most paramount principles in knowing the Holy Spirit as a person is knowing that as the Spirit of Truth, He will speak only truth to you:

However, when He, the Spirit of truth, has come, He will guide you into all truth; for He will not speak on His own authority, but whatever He hears He will speak; and He will tell you things to come (John 16:13).

Have you ever questioned, "Is what I'm hearing truly the Holy Spirit speaking to me?" To answer that question, Jesus promises, *"He will guide you into all truth."* This implies that without Him, we are limited in our ability to know God's perfect will.

For that weakness of ours, He is sent to us in order to accompany us in our decisions. He will lavish upon you the confident security that you need not fear in moments of apprehension that the choices you make are His.

I'll always remember the very first time the Holy Spirit taught me to trust His answer and heavenly guidance. The ministry I was involved with at the time was traveling to the Holy Land. It was a burning desire of my heart to go, but everything in the natural made it appear totally impossible. All I had was the "nonrefundable" down payment. If I submitted the deposit and had no way to get the balance, I would have lost $200. At the time, $200 was as if $2,000. As I deliberated within myself, I wanted to be sure that it was God's will for me to go, not just my personal desire. I had no doubt if the Holy Spirit showed me it was God's will, He would also take care of everything else.

One day I sat down at my kitchen table with my Bible. Suddenly, I was inspired to lay hands on my Bible and pray, "Lord Jesus, You know going to Israel is the desire of my heart, but I do not want to take a step if it is not in Your perfect will. I ask You to send the Holy Spirit to guide me through the written Word which is Your Truth. You promised He would guide us into all truth."

I told the Lord I would believe and trust whatever Scripture He would give me. I would believe the Scripture He showed me to be exactly what He wanted. Then I opened my Bible and my eyes fell upon these words, *"I will enter into the lodgings of his borders, and into the forest of his Carmel"* (2 Kings 19:23 KJV).

I took those words off the pages of Scripture to be my answer. I immediately sent my deposit. A few weeks later, a distant relative paid the ticket for me without asking. She said, "The Lord told me to buy your ticket." I had no idea what was to follow. Someone else I didn't know well said, "Here's money for the clothes you will need for the trip."

That experience changed my life forever. From that day forward, whenever I needed to know God's decision on a matter, I inquired in His Word and He gave it. Throughout the years, I learned that *"He will guide you in all truth."* The Holy Spirit is our heavenly Navigator; if you seek His guidance, He will not fail to give it.

Acts 16:6-10 teaches us how the Holy Spirit cleared the confusion for Paul:

*Now when they had gone through Phrygia and the region of Galatia, they were forbidden by the Holy Spirit to preach the word in Asia. After they had come to Mysia, they tried to go into Bithynia, but the Spirit did not permit them. So passing by Mysia, they came down to Troas. And **a vision appeared to Paul in the night.** A man of Macedonia stood and pleaded with him, saying, "Come over to Macedonia and help us." Now after he had seen the vision, immediately we sought to go to Macedonia, **concluding that the Lord had called us to preach the gospel to them.***

Our aim should be to always walk in love and develop a Christlike character.

The Holy Spirit Can Be Easily Grieved

Do not grieve the Holy Spirit of God, by whom you were sealed for the day of redemption. Let all bitterness, wrath, anger, clamor, and evil speaking be put away from you, with all malice (Ephesians 4:30-31).

There is nothing more serious to me than grieving the Holy Spirit. The Greek word for "grieve" is *lupeo,* which means to sadden, distress, or offend. Though at times we sadden the Holy Spirit, our aim should be to always walk in love and develop a Christlike character. We may be unaware that unkind words, rash judgment toward others, or harboring a grudge against someone we feel wronged us can grieve the Holy Spirit. The Holy Spirit in His nature is as gentle as a dove, and we see that in Matthew 3:16, John 1:32, Mark 1:10, and Luke 3:22. He is never rude, unkind, or insulting. He is a gentleman.

> *...God is love, and he who abides in love abides in God, and God in him* (1 John 4:16).

In my own life, I have discovered that strife grieves the Holy Spirit more than anything I've ever encountered. Angry words, a haughty attitude, or harsh words that are not Christlike that come out of our mouth can block the anointing.

We abide in the anointing when we abide in love. Hence, anything that is not the love of God in us needs to go. It needs to be reckoned and crucified with Christ.

> *For those who live according to the flesh set their minds on the things of the flesh, but those who live according to the Spirit, the things of the Spirit. For to be carnally minded is death, but* **to be spiritually minded is life and peace.** *Because the carnal mind is enmity against God; for it is not subject to the law of God, nor indeed can be. So then,* **those who are in the flesh cannot please God** (Romans 8:5-8).

This is why the explanation from the context of Ephesians 4:30 is found in verse 31, *"Let all bitterness, wrath, anger, clamor, and evil speaking be put away from you, with all malice"* (Ephesians 4:31). This means that grieving the Holy Spirit happens when we speak unkindly about someone, gossip, or slander another.

Grieving the Holy Spirit can also erupt in our attitudes. Unforgiveness and arrogance can hinder His power in our lives. Paul taught this in Philippians 2:1-3:

> *Therefore if there is any consolation in Christ, if any comfort of love, if any fellowship of the Spirit, if any affection and mercy, fulfill my joy by being like-minded, having the same love, being of one accord, of one mind. Let nothing be done through selfish ambition or conceit, but in lowliness of mind let each esteem others better than himself.*
>
> *For where envy and self-seeking exist, confusion and every evil thing are there* (James 3:16).

Finally, Paul teaches us that the Holy Spirit is poured out in our hearts by love, *"...the love of God has been poured out in our hearts by the Holy Spirit who was given to us"* (Romans 5:5).

Grieving the Holy Spirit does not mean you lose the anointing. However, it becomes blocked. We can feel His presence again even double more than before if we are willing to accept His grace and work on those behaviors that are inconsistent with the atmosphere of Heaven.

The Holy Spirit is the Voice of Jesus to You

> *While Peter thought about the vision, **the Spirit said to him,** "Behold, three men are seeking you"* (Acts 10:19).

> *As they ministered to the Lord and fasted, **the Holy Ghost said,** "Now separate to Me Barnabas and Saul for the work to which I have called them"* (Acts 13:2).

> *When he had come to us, he took Paul's belt, bound his own hands and feet, and said, **"Thus says the Holy Spirit,** 'So shall the Jews at Jerusalem bind the man who owns this belt, and deliver him into the hands of the Gentiles'"* (Acts 21:11).

The Holy Spirit is not limited to audible words when He speaks to us. He does this at times without uttering a sound through bearing witness in our conscience. This witness of the Spirit of God within us is the inaudible voice of God.

> *I tell the truth in Christ, I am not lying, my conscience also bearing me witness in the Holy Spirit* (Romans 9:1).

> *...And it is the Spirit who bears witness, because the Spirit is truth* (1 John 5:6).

Through the inward witness of the Spirit, we are led by the Spirit (Romans 8:14). Sometimes, He does this by prompting us. A thought will arise in our minds that is actually His instruction to us. For example, let's say someone went to church with you five years ago and you have not seen this person for a while, but keeps coming into your mind. Then perhaps people you see at work begin to remind you of that person. The individual's name and remembrance keep coming your way. This is one of the ways He prompts us. The way to respond would be to call the person right away, text, or go out of your way to seek out this individual. This is an assignment from the Holy Spirit. He wants someone to reach out to them, He wants you to follow His prompting.

Let's not be the ones who don't answer when He calls, *"...when I called, no one answered..."* (Isaiah 66:4). It is very important that when the Holy Spirit begins to show you someone's face or you think of that person that you submit immediately. Sometimes He will lead you to help someone, this means that we must act at the time He directs it.

An individual who trusts Him and wants to follow Him will consider the prompting a priority. This means you know that the prompting you sensed within was the Voice, without words leading you in a specific action. He wanted someone to respond to Him.

Let me tell you about a particular incident that involves following the leading of the Holy Spirit and acting immediately. It is another story from my missionary travels to China.

Many years ago, an assistant of mine cut out an article from the *Orange County Times*. It was about a man of God who was incarcerated for twenty-two years in Canton, China. This particular man of God was never given a trial. After years of living in the deplorable conditions of Mao Zedong's prison and surviving only on one bowl of unhusked rice per day, he developed cancer.

The newspaper article said this man was moved out of the prison in Canton to Hong Kong to receive treatment for cancer. Authorities decided to release him for treatment because of pressure from international human rights organizations that heard of his condition and insisted that he be treated.

When I read the article, I felt the fire and compassion of God well up within me. I could not shake it. I decided to go to Hong Kong again to seek out the man of God. All I knew was his name; I had no other connection with him whatsoever. I felt in my spirit that if I could lay hands on him, I knew he would be healed. This was not because of anything I have of myself. This is because of who Jesus is and what He did for us by dying on the Cross.

Within a few weeks, I landed in Hong Kong. I was very sure the compassion I felt in my heart was from the Holy Spirit speaking to me. The number-one problem I faced was where to find this man. The other challenge was that I only had a few hours in Hong Kong due to pending engagements in other countries during the duration of my trip out of the United States.

I arrived at the hotel at about 9 p.m. I prayed earnestly. How could I possibly locate someone I was not even sure was still in Hong Kong? For some reason, I opened the desk drawer located near the bed. In it was the Chinese version of Yellow Pages. Very few words were in English. As I thumbed through the thin pages, I felt "prompted" to look in the section that listed churches. These were identifiable to me because many of the names were in English. I continued to pray. I began to pray in tongues, then it came to me to call the churches associated with his denomination. There were so many that I didn't know which one to choose.

While praying, my hands and eyes seemed to be directed to one number in particular. I asked the operator to connect me to it. After several rings, a voice answered. I said, "Sir, do you speak English?"

He responded, "A little," in a thick accent.

"May I ask you a favor, sir? I have come all the way from the United State looking for the man who was recently brought here to get treatment for cancer after twenty-two years of incarceration for Christ."

He instantly knew who I was referring to. There was dead silence for a moment on the other side of the phone. Then he said, "How did you know I am the only one in Hong Kong looking after him? I was just visiting him in the hospital." He gave me instructions to take a taxi to meet him in thirty minutes on the steps of the hospital.

I quickly grabbed my purse and hailed a taxi. He met me on the steps and I was escorted up to the room. As they pulled the canvas back, he was sitting up in his bed waiting for me. They had quickly informed him of my coming. I took out the anointing oil and we prayed.

I didn't know what had become of him after that night until a year later. The next summer, my itinerary brought me again to Hong Kong. Upon inquiring, I found he was a resident at YahWan College. I visited him there with my staff. He was completely healed of cancer.

In Conclusion

Jesus introduced the Holy Spirit as a Person, and John includes that dissertation in three chapters. This teaches us that the Holy Spirit is given to us as a personal Helper, Guide, Comforter, and close Companion.

Companionship with the Holy Spirit can be quenched and thwarted through strife, a haughty attitude, or resentment fueled by unforgiveness toward another person in our heart. This can impede His gifts and supernatural works in us.

We can trust His word as a personal guide to our decisions, actions, or anything that concerns the future. If our walk with Christ seeks to emulate God's love, we can be sure the anointing will reach the summit for our destiny.

Closing Prayer

Dear Holy Spirit,

I want You to be my closest Companion. I fully surrender my thoughts, words, and deeds to You. I desire that Your power will lead me in a walk that is completely under Your guidance. Teach me not to grieve You. Give me the patience and kindness necessary to walk in love. I claim a new power and fresh anointing that will affect everyone I encounter on a daily basis. Teach me how to be led and prompted by the witness of Your presence within me. Amen.

About the Author

Dr. Michelle Corral is the founder of Breath of the Spirit Ministries International based in Orange County, California. She preaches and teaches each week at multiple campus locations throughout California and various Schools of the Prophets nationwide. In 2009, Dr. Corral launched Chesed International, which has built water wells, established daily feeding and education programs for children, staffed and financed medical missions worldwide, and provides refugee relief.

Her weekly telecast, *The Prophetic Word*, has aired on The Church Channel, The Inspirational Network, and is currently broadcast on The Word Network. Throughout the years, Dr. Corral has also been seen on TBN's classic programs *Praise the Lord, This is Your Day* with Pastor Benny and Suzanne Hinn, *The Threshing Floor* with Dr. Juanita Bynum, and many more.

Dr. Corral considers her ministry fruit of the legacy left by Kathryn Kuhlman.